smart toys

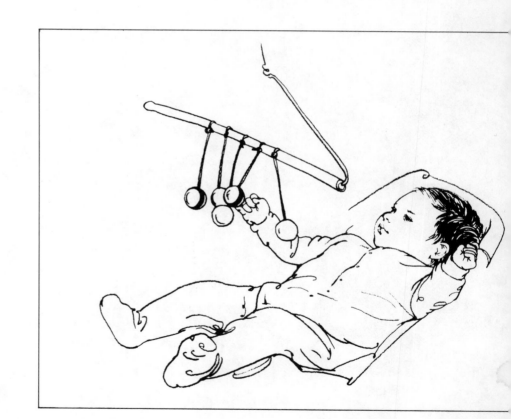

HARPER COLOPHON BOOKS

Harper & Row, Publishers, New York
Cambridge, Hagerstown, Philadelphia, San Francisco,
London, Mexico City, São Paulo, Sydney

smart toys

For Babies from Birth to Two

Kent Garland Burtt and Karen Kalkstein

Illustrations by Eulala Conner

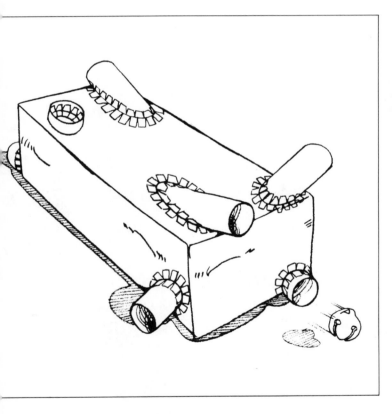

In this book many ideas in the essays on child development and many of the toy designs are based on the research findings of the Harvard Preschool Project which was directed by Burton L. White, Ph.D.

FIRST EDITION

Designer: Drawing Board Art Studio

Library of Congress Cataloging in Publication Data

Burtt, Kent Garland.
  Smart toys.
  (Harper colophon books)
  1. Infants. 2. Toys. 3. Child development.
4. Play. I. Kalkstein, Karen. II. Conner, Eulala.
III. Title.
HQ774.B87 1981   649'.55   80–8711
ISBN 0–06–090860–2 (pbk.)   AACR2

83 84 85 10 9 8 7 6 5 4

To our babies
Shelley, Forbes, Tina, Melissa, Kendall, and Jed
and to their fathers—Carleton and Shawn
who enriched their early years

Contents

Introduction

A father and mother are a baby's first teachers. They are responsible for providing from the very beginning of life the experiences that promote the growth of the child's mind as well as his body. Many of these experiences will naturally include toys, and toys geared carefully to an infant's skills will help you to teach your baby. This book shows you how to construct interesting toys and how to introduce them so your baby derives the maximum benefit from them.

Your child-rearing style during the period from birth to 2 years of age deeply influences your child's personality and intellect. Never again will you get the chance to have such an impact on his attitudes toward learning. The many facts in this book about baby and toddler interests and abilities will help you develop a style of parenting that will bring out your child's full potential.

WHY MAKE YOUR OWN TOYS

Scientists and educational researchers have recently made discoveries about infant behavior that offer guidelines for the design and presentation of playthings. Our toy models are based on these discoveries. You can't find many suitable things in stores because toy manufacturers haven't yet taken advantage of the behavioral studies. Often expensive items are ignored by a baby or are inappropriate to the age level they are sold for.

The scientific research conducted in homes and laboratories has uncovered what really appeals to a baby at each successive phase of development. These findings are reflected in the visual, audio, and tactile details of our toy prototypes. The toys you make from our patterns will be more attractive to your infant than most commercial ones, giving his touch feedback in the form of noise or movement. The educational success of a toy is measured by a baby's interest in it. If he's interested in it, he's going to investigate it visually and manually. And inevitably he learns from his investigations.

Making toys at home will save you a lot of money. Today commercial toys have high price tags. Infant toys seem especially expensive because they are appropriate for only a few weeks or, at best, a few months. Infant skills and interests change rapidly.

You will undoubtedly get a special fascination from watching your baby react to something you yourself have built. This pleasure can easily beat the experience of giving a store-bought toy.

Making your baby's toys will inspire you to observe his behaviors more closely and think more carefully about his stages of development and individuality. After you've made a toy, we give you hints on how to set the stage for your baby's experience with it. Often his first efforts at playing with a toy are clumsy, but as he continues, his handling of it becomes adept. This process is exciting to witness.

We hope you will take the modest amount of time necessary to make many of the toys in this book. Offering them to your baby will make the first 2 years more educational for him and more interesting and fun for you.

EDUCATING YOUR BABY WITH TOYS

At what distance from a young baby's eyes should you place a colorful object? How do you rig up a toy securely enough so an early reacher, lying on her back, can grab it, let it go, and then find it still over her head a few minutes later? What kinds of play encourage problem-solving skills in the toddler? Answers to these questions appear in the chapters that follow.

The type of toy a young baby is most likely to interact with changes every few weeks. The trick is to match the plaything to the currently emerging skill. Each new skill is a landmark. As early as the first week a baby focuses intently and even tracks a moving object. At 8 weeks she bats or swipes at things dangling over her hands. Later she reaches, holds, pulls. Wow! Watching the progress is spellbinding.

As designer of the environment, the parent or caregiver presents the toy that gives the baby a reason to exercise her ability of the moment. Here's how the sequence begins: first a bold graphic to look at; next a clicking or clinking toy to bat; then a steady, nearby object to grab.

Interesting play materials for the older baby keep her from clinging too much to you, from getting bored, or from getting into mischief. They ease her through that period of negativism before independence at 2 years. An involved toddler, engrossed in materials, seldom requires discipline. As your child learns to crawl, cruise, climb, and walk you can provide homemade equipment that invites her to exercise these skills. For instance, when she first begins to climb, she will be magnetically drawn to the ramp and stairs of heavy cardboard described in this book (Climb and Slide Fun, Chapter Four).

The hours she spends staring at and manipulating small, intriguingly shaped objects will amaze you. We suggest numerous items (many of them household cast-offs) to practice finger skills on. The toddler's fascination with containers, mirrors, hinged objects, locks, balls, things that move, water, sand, and paper inspired many of our toy designs.

All our items feed innate curiosity—that precious quality which all babies are born with and which later becomes the incentive for good performance at school. (Sometimes, unfortunately, curiosity is stifled at an early age by parents who overprotect or confine their child too closely, thereby not permitting her to satisfy her instinct to explore.) Some of our toys encourage a talent for problem-solving—an aptitude that starts to blossom after about 7 months of age.

LAYETTE SHOULD INCLUDE TOYS

Furnishing the nest properly for the newborn means providing equipment for playtime as well as bath time and bedtime. A proper layette should include not only a wardrobe of clothes but also of toys. In the early months you should attach attractive toys to the bassinet, crib, playpen, car seat, or bed, and place them near the infant seat. Playthings can be loose in bed or on a mat for the baby who creeps. It's a good idea to construct many of the first toys while you are pregnant so they will be ready when the baby comes. You can make toys for the older months after the birth.

The making of educational toys is a good outlet for modern moms-to-be who don't take naturally to knitting booties. And it gives prospective fathers the chance they want to get involved. An older brother or sister can help put toys together and then have fun observing the small sibling's reactions. You may also wish to make some of the playthings in this book to give as presents to friends who are expecting a baby.

EASY TO MAKE

You don't have to be clever at crafts to make use of this book. The playthings are easy to construct and take only a short time to assemble. They are grouped according to the age of the baby. Drawings show you stages of construction and what the final product should look like. The needed materials, listed for each toy, are either common household items or inexpensive products available at hardware and stationery stores. The step-by-step instructions are simple to follow. The reason for each toy is explained. Suggestions as to how to present the toy to your baby are included and ways to vary the pattern and play experience are sometimes mentioned.

MONITORING YOUR BABY'S LEARNING

Facilitating an infant's involvement with toys is a role that appeals to contemporary parents, many of whom may think of feeding, diaper-changing, dressing, and bathing as boring routines. However, they can become quite engrossed in monitoring the cognitive development of their infant. This takes brains; it's challenging work for thinking parents. Often their ingenuity is responsible for their baby's constant excitement about the world around him. And an habitual mood of enthusiasm in a baby promotes good-naturedness and sociability.

Alert observation helps you get to know your baby's personality and gives you cues as to what he's ready for next. (Sometimes watch him play from a position where you are hidden from his view because, if you appear, he may stop studying or playing with the toy to look at you.)

Remember: babies are different, even those in the same family. Not all will like every toy in this book. Babies reveal their individualities in toy preferences. The toy that rivets the attention of one may go practically unnoticed by another, so you have to experiment. A baby's particular inclinations will facilitate his enjoyment of a specific toy. For example, a constant kicker will contact a kick toy at the foot of his bed faster than a baby who lies quietly most of the time. Discover your baby's taste in toys.

If your baby doesn't pay any attention to something you have just spent your time and energy making, don't be discouraged. Perhaps he's tired. Try it again when he's in a different mood. Give him a few days to catch on to how to interact with it. And a toy will often merchandise itself. Its presence gradually elicits from the baby the behaviors that will enable him to get a lot of pleasure out of it.

Our toys are categorized according to a broad age range, but your baby may be interested in a particular toy sooner or later than the calendar months given. In general, we place a toy in as young an age bracket as would be at all reasonable. This is done to assure that the toy is ready in time for your baby to derive maximum enjoyment from it. It would be disappointing to make a toy and find out your baby had outgrown it. The age at which babies are ready for a certain type of toy varies. If your baby seems indifferent to a just-finished creation, wait a week and introduce it again.

Your child may continue to derive pleasure from toys past the age bracket they're assigned to. This is to be expected in some cases. But when we think a child might break a toy if he uses it at an older age and hurt himself, we urge you to put such a toy away.

CHILD APPEAL

Realize that the early toys are constructed to look "pretty" from the infant's point of view, not the adult's. For instance, it is only the underside of each part of a mobile that is seen by a baby looking up from her mattress. Many commercial mobiles have objects with attractive profiles, making them interesting only to the adult standing beside the crib.

Few people realize that pale pink and light blue, the traditional baby colors, do not attract the glance of a baby. Research has revealed that the contrast of black on white and the garish shades of red or shocking pink are more likely to arrest a baby's attention.

A toy that moves is usually more fascinating than one that doesn't. Wherever possible the feature of movement has been built into a model.

You can also enhance the appeal of a toy by a slight alteration of it once the baby has become used to its original form. For example, wrapping a piece of yellow tape around a favorite red ball changes that familiar object; the baby's interest in it is renewed. Look for our suggestions on possible variations. Or you can use your imagination in periodically adding or subtracting details to a basic design. A model of each of our toys has been played with by babies, and each one has been enjoyed.

KEEP YOUR BABY COMPANY

Of course your presence as loving playmate is far more valuable than the proximity of an inanimate object, however colorful. Your voice and facial expressions reflect your feelings and respond instantaneously to the baby's efforts at communication. Face-to-face exchanges are vital to normal development as a social being.

But when you are at work or busy at home with chores, the toys are there to teach about the physical world and to advance development. They have power to awaken the baby's interest in his surroundings, nourish his curiosity, and reinforce his desire to figure things out. At times the toys even ward off crying by curing infant boredom and fretfulness or by distracting from toddler crankiness.

Early childhood researchers have discovered that well-developing babies actually spend a greater proportion of their time playing with physical objects than they do interacting with their parents. However, the few seconds you spend expressing delight with your child who has just fit a lid to a container are just as important as the many minutes he spends trying to fit it. He needs your personal reactions to his climactic moments of defeat or triumph.

IF YOU ARE WORKING

If you have a part- or full-time job, you don't have to leave your infant's education to chance. Share this book with the caregiver you've employed for your child. Since these first years are so important, see to it that he or she is familiar with the approaches to play described in this book. In everyday language discuss your child's current stage of development together. Talk over with that person specifics such as how to vary the crib toys or how to work with your toddler's collection of small objects. When you return from work, you might ask for a description of your child's reactions that day to a certain toy. If interviewing a prospective caregiver, you might feel out his or her receptivity to ideas about educationally oriented babysitting.

SAFETY FIRST

Any toy you make or buy has to be inspected with safety criteria in mind. Also, any household object you give your baby has to be screened. Look out for sharp points or edges. Wooden things have to be sanded smoothly to prevent splinters. Any object smaller than 1¼ inches in diameter and 2¼ inches in depth could be swallowed. Examine larger objects to be sure they do not have too-small parts that could be pried off, screwed off, or broken off. Babies after 4 months have increasing strength in their hands and vigorous ways of manipulating objects. Also beware of substances that could flake off or crumble when mouthed or chewed. Nontoxic paint and nontoxic glue are musts when making toys.

For a young baby who cannot sit up to have access to toys, they must be suspended above her head. However, every precaution must be taken to make sure these toys have no small parts that could fall off and be ingested by an infant. When constructing toys, use extra care to make them properly, even if this takes you extra time. Also, position them correctly and securely. Your carefulness is an insurance against accident.

If an older child lives in your home or visits you, special caution must be taken. He might damage a toy, through a different kind of handling than it was designed for, leaving it unsafe for the baby. If the older child is mature enough to make the toys with you, he will be more understanding of the care to be exercised with them.

We have sprinkled Safety Notes throughout the book. Please heed them. They alert you to unlikely but potential hazards to an infant regarding play materials given her. We have designed the toys to be as safe as possible, but we urge precautions such as double-checking from time to time that the glue, epoxy, or cloth tape is still holding the toys together. Occasionally we recommend supervision when your baby plays with a particular toy.

A BOOK FOR PARENT EDUCATORS

Grandparents and occasional baby-sitters, as well as full-time caregivers, may profitably dip into the following pages. Also sharing the responsibility for education of the infant these days are parent educators, family counselors, day-care center personnel, and home teachers in early education projects. This book can also help them in their work. Mainly it is written as an aid to mothers and fathers eager to enrich their baby's surroundings with playthings designed for his entertainment and development.

Materials to Collect and Useful Tools

If you plan to make many of the toys in this book, you might start to collect the items listed below. This is not an exhaustive list, but it includes materials you will use in more than one toy.

"Raw" materials (items you will probably have to purchase)

Paper goods

white poster board
crepe paper
tissue paper
construction paper, in bright colors
colored cellophane
white typing or drawing paper
Con-Tact paper: transparent, brightly colored plain, or patterned
gift and brown wrapping paper
paper towels and napkins

Wood

various pieces of plywood, ⅜″ thick, cut to sizes as specified in instructions

Sewing Materials

fabric remnants in plain and patterned styles and of various textures
scraps of black and white felt
polyester pillow and quilt filling
dress elastic
heavy waistband elastic

Velcro fasteners
ribbons, various colors: buy them or cut them from fabric
   remnants with pinking shears
buttons, large, various styles
thread, regular weight and heavy black

Household items (objects you probably have around the home)

Boxes

cylindrical oatmeal boxes
cylindrical salt boxes
sliding match boxes
corrugated cartons
shoe boxes
gift boxes in assorted sizes

Plastic containers

empty plastic bottles (shampoo, detergent)
large Clorox bottle

Paper goods

newspapers
greeting cards
old magazines
used bags, envelopes
shirt cardboards
empty toilet-paper and paper-towel rolls

Balls

old tennis balls
Ping-Pong balls
any other kinds, except very small ones

Miscellaneous

colored sponges
aluminum foil
tin cans, various sizes
spoons: wooden, plastic (serving size), and measuring sets
sleigh bells
hanging plant hooks
suction-cup hooks
wire clothes hangers, with and without cardboard roll
dried beans, split peas, popcorn kernels, and peanuts

Materials to Collect and Useful Tools

For decorating

felt-tip pens with nontoxic permanent ink, various colors
nontoxic crayons, various colors
nontoxic acrylic paint, bright colors: water-based acrylics come in tubes at art supply stores

For attaching

Tapes

cloth tape, of various widths (Mystik): buy in assorted widths or cut wider rolls to desired widths with pinking shears or scissors
plastic tape (Scotch): an alternative to cloth tape but not quite as strong and durable
masking tape
transparent tape (Scotch)

For tying or hanging

light- and heavyweight string
yarn, various colors, regular and extra-strong weight
ribbons, various colors: buy them or cut them from fabric remnants with pinking shears

Adhesives

Elmer's Glue-All, or other nontoxic white glue
epoxy

Useful tools

This is a list of tools that will be helpful to you in making certain toys described in this book.

scissors
pinking shears
ruler
mat knife or single-edged razor blade
ice pick
knitting needle
drill (hand or electric)
paper punch
sandpaper
steel wool
large paper clips
large rubber bands
paint brush
needle

Chapter One

Birth to 1½ Months: Learning Comes from Looking

EDUCATION

Babies start learning from day 1. They learn faster and become more intelligent if the bassinet area is enriched with interesting things to look at and listen to. If there is nothing nearby but empty space and a plain pastel bassinet lining, then there is little nourishment for the growth of the baby's mind.

Babies need sensory stimuli; that is, nearby objects that stimulate their sense of sight and hearing. Just as parents supply the right food for their baby's physical hunger, so they should provide the right type and amount of nourishment for their baby's cognitive appetite.

Correctly positioned playthings give your baby the incentive to exercise the amazing abilities she has to see and hear in the first weeks of life and, later, to touch as well. Exercise of these abilities naturally advances mental and physical development.

There are certain developmental landmarks of the first half year such as batting, hands-to-midline clasping, and reaching and grasping. These landmarks will occur earlier than is average if you provide pictures and mobiles to look at during the first 6 weeks, then toys to touch after that. The sooner your baby is actively using her early skills of seeing, hearing, and touching, the sooner these skills will be teaching her about her world. And the sooner she learns, the smarter she'll get.

Babies in the first month can see quite adequately things placed near their eyes. Having bold, bright pictures to focus on makes them more alert and attentive for a greater number of seconds than babies without such visual enrichment. Babies who are alert and attentive, even if only for brief periods, will advance faster than drowsy babies who are not stimulated during their awake moments.

Later, babies who are supplied with 3-dimensional objects to touch right where their hands are waving about will learn to bat and grasp things sooner than babies without touchable play-things nearby. The babies with toys are at an advantage because their sense of touch teaches them much about their physical world.

BEHAVIORS

It seems your round-the-clock snoozer is seldom awake except for feedings. So what time is there for toys? At 4 weeks he averages a grand total of 6 or 7 minutes of alertness an hour. That's not much, but it is enough to benefit from some visual enrichment. Take advantage of these short periods to show him a toy from your collection. Or you may leave one ideally placed inside the bassinet for him to notice upon awakening.

When lying on his back, a new baby always turns his head toward the side of his bed, usually the right side. So fasten a toy to the side of the bassinet or prop it up on the mattress against the wicker. Don't hang it overhead.

A tiny baby is more likely to open his eyes and keep them open in a dimly lit room than in a brightly lit one or outdoors. So lower the shades a bit to encourage your baby to notice playthings.

A newborn's hands stay in a fisted position. Although he can momentarily clasp a rattle, this time-honored toy is not educationally important in the first few months.

ABILITIES

At this age your baby's major way of interacting with toys is simply to look at them. She can see things placed at any point between 7 and 24 inches from her eyes, but focuses best on an object 7 to 9 inches away. She can sometimes follow a large, colorful object moving slowly above her.

The parent or caregiver is in the business of giving the baby opportunities to exercise these visual abilities. So provide things that she will like to look at. This first chapter contains patterns for things known to appeal to very young babies.

INTERESTS

A baby loves to stare at the face of the person holding him. He zeroes in on the eyes more than any other facial feature. He also likes pictures of faces.

A new baby will notice various abstract patterns such as diagonal lines or a checkerboard or target design traced in sharply contrasting colors, especially black on white. Our pattern called Art Gallery tells you how to assemble these. But a newborn prefers the shape of the human face to any other illustration, abstract or realistic. We start your baby off with a drawing of a face. The pattern for it is called Face to Face.

The uninitiated parent is more likely to give his or her baby too few rather than too many things to look at within the infant focal range. Don't be concerned that several things in the bassinet will overexcite him.

An infant has a strong interest in variety; change the "scenery" every few days. After you've offered all the toys in the first section of this book, make up your own variations. The possibilities are numerous. Also work ahead, so that you have completed some of the toys in the second chapter by the time your baby reaches that second stage of development.

In the challenging process of adjusting to life itself, a new baby seems mostly interested in getting physically comfortable. He spends much of the time that he's not asleep seeking relief from the discomforts of hunger, overeating, indigestion, a wet or dirty diaper, gas, or difficulties with the breast or bottle nipple. Always answering his cries (without any concern for spoiling him)

may seem all you can manage. But you will have some special fun if you look for optimum moments to present your baby with the graphics and mobiles suggested in this first chapter, and then observe his reaction.

Don't worry if these toys don't seem to "work" every time you introduce them. Be patient and keep trying. As a general rule, wait until your baby is at peace to show him a toy. However, if he has been fed, changed, and burped and is still fussing, hold up a picture or jiggle a mobile. His fretting could result from sheer boredom or the need to focus on something other than the state of his body. Singing to him might help or playing soft classical music; rocking him or pacing the room with him in your arms can also have a soothing effect.

Gradually, as comfort becomes a condition he can take for granted, your baby becomes much more interested in the colorful world around him. You can probably count on real readiness to explore visually the bassinet environs at some point between 1 and 2 months of age.

1. Face to Face

Reason for Toy

New babies prefer a simple picture of the human face to any other pattern shown them. When they see it, their eyes sometimes stop roving or looking vacant or sleepy. The eyes may widen and noticeably fix their attention on this picture for a number of seconds.

Around 6 weeks of age babies start liking faces with more visual detail such as those cut out from magazines. At 8 weeks babies smile readily when presented with a picture of a face.

Materials

white poster board
black felt-tip pen
Scotch transparent tape
lightweight string

Instructions

1. Cut an oval about 6″ x 7″ from poster board.
2. Draw a face showing hairline, omitting mouth. (Babies focus only on area from nose to hair.)
3. Cut a strip of poster board 3″ x ½″. Fold it to create a picture hook (a). Tape it lengthwise to center back of oval.
4. Thread a string through hook and tie it (b).

How to Use

Thread the string through the bassinet wicker and tie the face to the right side of the bassinet. The ideal distance is 7″ to 9″ from your baby's eyes.

If the bed is lined, tie string around bassinet rim and dangle face down inside until it touches the mattress. Or simply prop it up on the mattress without string.

Keep an extra face in the kitchen. Just hold it up to your baby, eyeball to eyeball occasionally, and observe her reaction. Her interest in it should grow and her glance last longer as she matures.

Variations

When your baby approaches 6 weeks, substitute this stylized face for a realistic one with more detail. You can cut a large, glamorous face out of a fashion magazine or an exotic face (no less than 4″ in diameter) out of a travel magazine. Your baby will continue to enjoy faces at 3 and 4 months of age, smiling and talking to them.

2. Holder for Bassinet Toys

Reason for Toy

Since babies in their early weeks can see—and enjoy seeing—objects placed within the focal distance of their eyes, you should plan an enriched bassinet environment. This entails rigging up a device to hold objects over the bassinet.

a

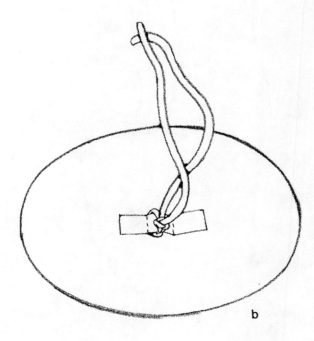

b

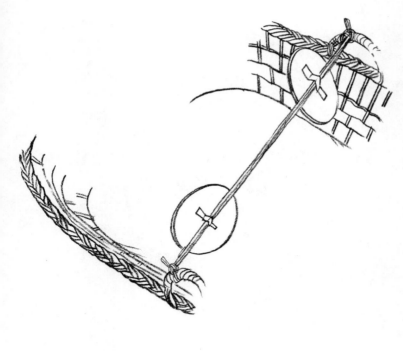

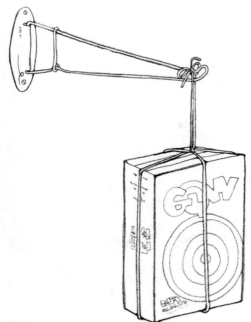

Materials

heavyweight string, about 12″ longer than the width of your bassinet, or dress elastic, ¼″ or ⅜″ wide and 12″ longer than
bassinet width (stretchiness of elastic enables you to give it
a tug and make the toys on it jiggle)

Instructions

1. Stretch a piece of string or dress elastic across your baby's
cradle or bassinet.
2. Fasten each end by slipping it through the wicker and knotting
it. If the rim and sides are solidly lined, extend the string or
elastic over both sides and down the outside of the bassinet.
(You'll need longer string or elastic.) Anchor it by tying it to
the legs or the stand on which the bassinet rests.
3. If you have only a portable basket, lay it between 2 pieces
of furniture to which you can fasten the ends of the string
or elastic.

How to Use

Place this holder across middle of bassinet, over approximate
middle of your baby's body, not directly above baby's head. Objects should hang 7″ to 9″ from the eyes of younger babies.
After 6 weeks any distance from 6″ to 12″ is fine.

Variations

Hanging plant hook: The support device for a hanging plant works
nicely as a holder for homemade mobiles. Screw it into the wall
near your baby's changing table or bassinet or in an area where
you place the infant seat. You can also buy an inexpensive suction-cup hook.

Hanger as holder: A wire clothes hanger can be used to
suspend pictures or objects. Hook it to the hood of your bassinet

or carriage, or hang it from a ceiling or wall light. You may have to tie one end of a string to your light and the other end to the hanger hook in order to lower the hanger's ornaments close to your baby.

You can also suspend the hanger from the handle of a closet or cupboard door which you open and swing out from the wall to better position toys in front of your baby.

3. Art Gallery

Reason for Toy

Babies can discriminate among patterns after they are 1 week old. To arrest the attention of newborns, patterns have to be made of sharply contrasting colors. Black on white makes the boldest design. Expect your baby to study these pictures most carefully between the ages of 6 and 8 weeks, but present them sooner.

Materials

white poster board
wide black felt-tip pen
photograph of a face (about 4″ x 6″), cut from a magazine
string
Scotch transparent tape

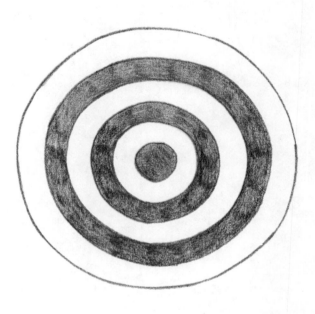

Instructions

1. Glue the magazine face to poster board. Cut out picture.
2. Cut an oval 4½″ x 6″ from poster board. Draw a simple face on it with pen.
3. Cut a circle of poster board about 5″ in diameter and draw thick concentric circles with pen.

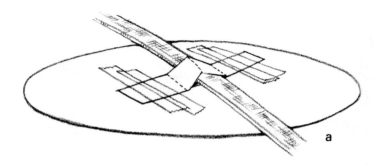

a

4. On the back of each of these pictures, tape a tab made of a little strip of poster board. Bend the tab to allow space for a string. Thread a piece of string through each tab (a).
5. Tie or thread pictures onto taut string or elastic holder across bassinet. (See previous pattern.) Perhaps only 2 pictures will fit across bassinet; tie one to the left of center and one to the right, remembering that your baby doesn't look directly overhead at this age. Prop other pictures on mattress or in car bed, or hold them up for your baby to see any time he's awake in your arms. (See variations below for more designs.)

How to Use

If your bassinet is very shallow, the pictures may hang too low to be in the baby's line of sight. If so, then prop them up on the mattress, leaning them against the wicker, or tie them to the wicker side.

You may also suspend pictures with string from a hanger. Now you have a mobile.

While a bassinet has a lot of charm, a crib is an easier place to arrange toys for viewing. You may wish to move your baby to one after the first month, at least for some periods of the day.

Variations

When your art fancier has begun to pay regular attention to his pictures, you could mount a new exhibit.

Diagonals: Cut a piece of white poster board 5½″ x 7″. With pen, draw and color in diagonal lines about ¾″ to 1″ wide and the same distance apart.

Checkerboard: Cut a square 5½″ x 5½″ from poster board and color in a checkerboard design.

Picasso face: Draw a face with moderate distortions—one eye big, the other small; or the eyes on different levels; or the mouth tilted and off center.

Keep these pictures on the holder until your baby is 2 months old. When he begins touching them, he'll make them spin like a paddle wheel. Switch their positions on the holder occasionally.

4. Shiny Pendants

Reason for Toy

At this period your baby is only in the business of looking when not nursing or sleeping. She will express interest in her world if her immediate environment contains some bright objects. Since your baby is looking at the bottoms of a mobile's ornaments, their undersides should be broad and shiny or colorful. The ideal age for mobiles is 3 to 9 weeks.

Materials

thin chain (from hardware store), the width of bassinet
metal mesh pot scrubber
4 foil tart pans, 5″ in diameter
heavyweight string
colorful yarn
Scotch transparent tape

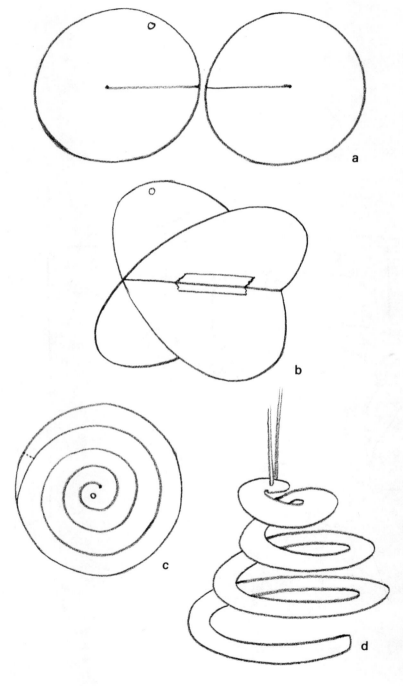

a

b

c

d

Instructions

1. Tie a length of string onto each end of chain for attaching it to bed. When you fasten the objects to chain, pair them toward either end so they'll be seen by a baby whose head is turned to the side.
2. Poke yarn through center of scrubber and hang it from one of links. Length of yarn depends on distance between bassinet rim and mattress. You want the objects to dangle about 7″ to 9″ from baby's eyes.
3. Punch 2 small holes in center bottom of 1 foil tart pan. String yarn through the holes so pan hangs upside down. (This yarn could be a different length from the first, bearing in mind baby's range of focus.) Tie yarn ends onto another link.
4. Cut out the bottom circles of 2 other tart pans. Slit each from the edge to the center and punch a small hole farther along the edge of one (a). Slide the slits into each other. Keep the circles at right angles to each other with bits of tape applied where the circles intersect (b). Thread yarn through hole and hang at opposite end of chain from last pendant.
5. Cut out bottom circle of another pan. Starting from edge, cut a spiral (c). Stretch it out (d). Make hole in center for yarn. Thread yarn and tie to a link near last object.

How to Use

Place chain across bassinet or crib. If mattress depth is shallow, perhaps your baby will see pendants better if you attach chain along one side of bed.

If she is lying on the floor, you could attach mobile to the handles of a nearby chest of drawers, or to a chair and move chair close to baby's right side.

Safety Note

Hang mobile out of reach after your baby is 8 weeks old. This mobile has some sharp edges and is not meant to be touched or pulled.

5. Bull's-Eye Mobile

Reason for Toy

Researchers have found that the design babies prefer to look at, second to a picture of the human face, is the pattern of a target. The black-and-white contrasting concentric circles hold a strong fascination for them.

Materials

3 Styrofoam balls, 2″ or more in diameter (big enough not to be swallowed)
black and/or dark green or red acrylic or other nontoxic paint
wire clothes hanger, with cardboard roll left on
lightweight string
cloth tape (optional), in red and black

Instructions

1. On each ball paint a variation of a target design which can be enjoyed from the underside as well as broadside (a).
2. Cut 3 lengths of string 12″ long.
3. With a knitting needle or ice pick, poke string all the way through centers of each ball and out the other side (b).
4. Tie several knots in the end of the strings so they won't pull back through the balls.
5. Cut 3 grooves in the cardboard roll on hanger and tie each string around roll where grooves are (c). Balls should dangle down about 7″ to 9″ from baby's eyes.
6. Optional: If you have no paint, you can cut 1¼″ strips and make designs on balls with tape instead. You can also cover cardboard roll with colored tape or paint it for added color interest.

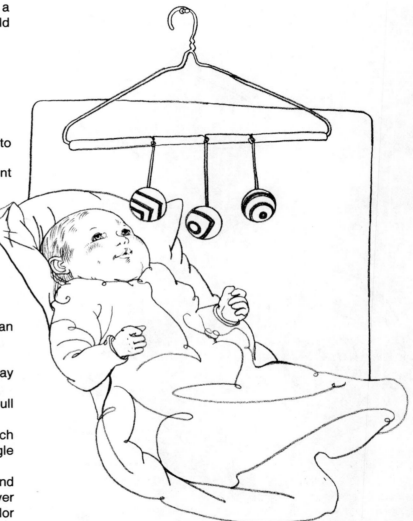

6. Stained-Glass Mobile

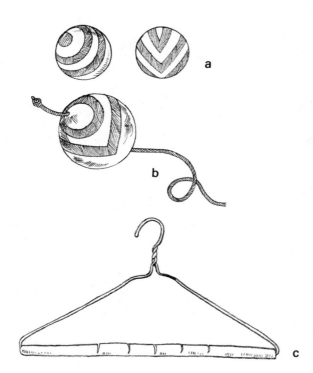

Reason for Toy

Most commercial mobiles have objects that hang vertically so that they look pretty from the adult consumer's point of view who sees them from a standing position beside the crib. This mobile is designed to appeal to the infant who sees it from underneath.

Materials

wire clothes hanger
several sheets of black construction paper
various shades of colored cellophane (or transparent polystyrene sheet protectors from stationery store or Saran Wrap and colored felt-tip pens)*
heavy black thread and needle
Elmer's Glue-All
1 push-pin tack

How to Use

Hang mobile from bassinet or carriage hood. Hook it to knob of kitchen cabinet over counter space where your baby rests in his infant seat. Bring it along to grandmother's house or a friend's apartment.

Safety Note

This mobile is only for looking. It can withstand only gentle motion during the early days of your baby's batting stage. Then put it away; it is not sturdy enough to withstand grasping or pulling. Balls might come off and they shouldn't be sucked because Styrofoam crumbles easily.

Instructions

1. Lay one sheet of black paper on top of another and cut out 5 or 6 geometric shapes (a). The overall size can vary between 3½" and 7".
2. Cut out the centers, leaving each shape as a black frame about ½" wide.
3. Smear a thin layer of glue over inside of one frame. Glue this to a piece of cellophane. Put glue on inside of matching frame and glue it also to same piece of cellophane between the 2 identical frames (b). Follow this procedure with each shape.

---

* If you cannot find colored cellophane, you can make your own by coloring sheet protectors or pieces of Saran Wrap. Color the plastic with bright-colored permanent felt-tip pens. Color one side. Let it dry. Then turn and color other side with same pen for a deep stained-glass look.

4. Bend hanger into a square and raise hook to stand at right angle to the square. Hang it on a push-pin stuck in a bulletin board or wall. (This position is for attaching the ornaments properly; later take it to wherever the baby is lying.)
5. Now thread your needle with a long piece of thread and knot the end. Sew through a corner of one of the shapes. Then, leaving about 6″ of thread length for dangling, tie the thread around the hanger wire with a couple of knots (c). Then come back down with your needle and sew through an opposite corner of your shape, making thread lengths even so shape hangs horizontally. Knot thread and cut off excess.
6. Attach all frames to hanger with thread of differing lengths. Hang most of the shapes on the horizontal for your baby's benefit. For variety, a couple of shapes can hang vertically by just a single length of thread. One shape can even be hung from another. (See illustration at beginning of this chapter.)

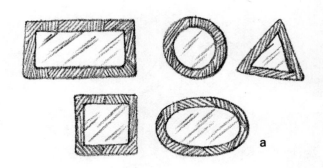

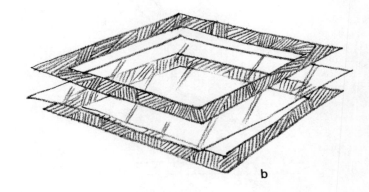

How to Use

Hang mobile 8″ to 12″ from your baby's eyes, perhaps from carriage hood. If necessary, in order to lower the mobile closer to the baby, tie a string to the hanger hook. Then tie the other end of the string to a wall sconce or hanging plant hook.

These shapes should sway with the slightest movement of air. Let them catch the light of a window or lamp, if possible. Also try for a position where they may also throw patches of color on the bassinet lining or a nearby white wall.

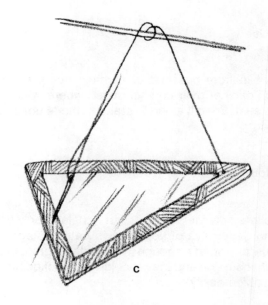

Safety Note

Keep mobile out of baby's reach or put away once she starts to touch. This mobile is only for looking. Preschoolers should not handle it because it is quite delicate.

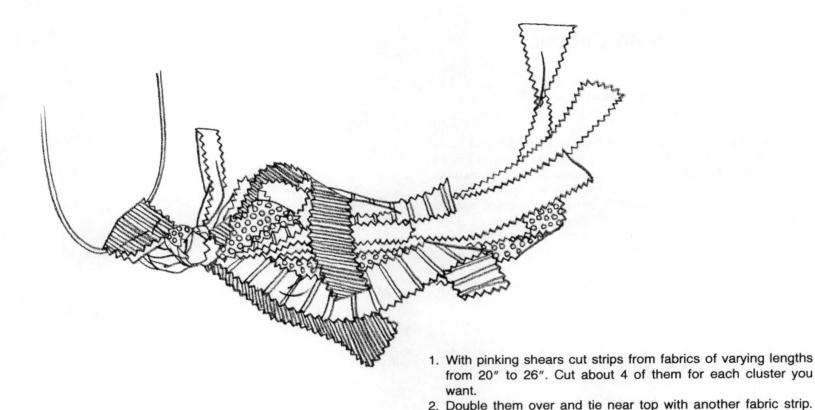

1. With pinking shears cut strips from fabrics of varying lengths from 20″ to 26″. Cut about 4 of them for each cluster you want.
2. Double them over and tie near top with another fabric strip.

7. Fluttering Ribbons

How to Use

Hang ribbons to the right or left 12″ from baby's eyes. Suspend over bassinet, from handle of kitchen cabinet, over changing table, or, best of all, near open window or outside on carriage hood. An electric fan blowing on them has a dramatic effect.

Reason for Toy

Babies like things that move. These ribbons dance in the breeze. At this stage the only way babies can entertain themselves is by watching things. They want and need a variety of spectacles. So here is another treat for their visual appetite.

Variation

Materials

Using your resources and imagination, find other objects to dangle from cabinet handle or hanging plant device. For example, hang a scarf, a brightly colored food box, or a paper party hat. (See illustration for Holder for Bassinet Toys.)

brightly colored, patterned fabrics or ribbons

Birth to 1½ Months: Learning Comes from Looking

8. Flying Saucer

Reason for Toy

A newborn can spot a large, brightly colored object and follow it with his eyes as you move it slowly in an arc above his head.

    This type of visual-pursuit toy has been used in laboratories where infant skills are tested. Try it and enjoy noticing one of the first skills your baby manifests: the ability to track a slowly moving object.

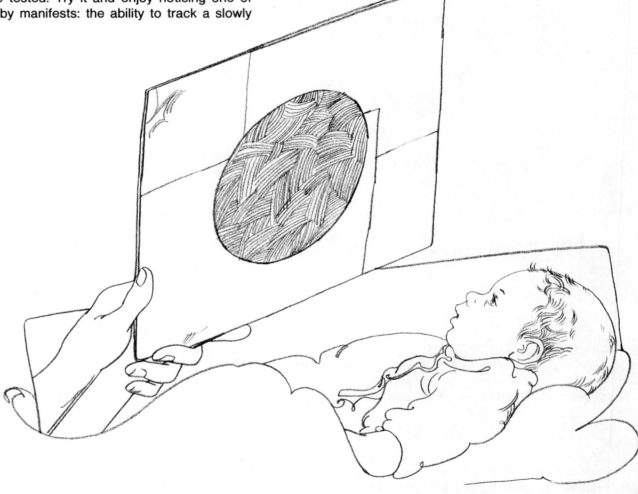

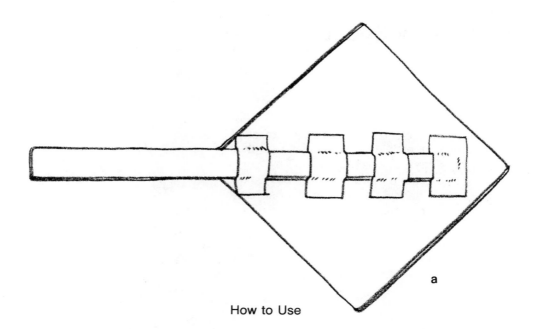

a

Materials

piece of lightweight cardboard
white paper (sheets of typing paper will do) or record sleeve
red construction paper
section of corrugated carton
Elmer's Glue-All
Scotch transparent tape
heavy masking tape

Instructions

1. Cut cardboard into a square 16″ x 14″.
2. Cover 1 side with white paper using glue or tape.
3. Cut a circle 7″ in diameter from red construction paper. Glue it in the center of the square.
4. From the side of a corrugated carton, cut a strip about 25″ x 2″. Tape it on the back of the square with masking tape, making a handle about 9″ long coming from 1 corner (a).

How to Use

Try this toy only when your baby is awake and quiet. Hold it to the side of his head about 12″ from his eyes. Shake it a little to get his attention. He will see it out of the corner of his eyes. Then move it through the air slowly (about 1 foot per second) in an arc above his head. If he loses sight of it, shake it again in the periphery of his visual field. He may follow it for only a few seconds. Recapture his attention as often as necessary. Performance will improve dramatically by 6 weeks of age. After that a baby will pursue a moving target repeatedly and with precision.

Variation

Make another large white square and glue a black felt or paper circle 3″ in diameter in the center. When your baby is 6 weeks old, hold it 36″ away from his eyes, then bring it slowly closer. At about 18″ from his eyes your baby will notice it and seem to follow it compulsively till it comes as close as 8″. Then he'll stop looking at it. The range at which he can see it increases over the next weeks. He notices it when 30″ away and follows it to as close as 4″.

9. Sunburst Sheet

Reason for Toy

Babies derive no benefit from looking at an expanse of solid white sheet. With this sheet under them, babies, lying on their tummy, have an interesting pattern at which to gaze. Tiny hands show up better against a background of contrasting color value, helping babies to notice their hands sooner. So choose dark shades to dye a sheet for a white baby and light shades for a black baby.

Materials

1 all-cotton white crib sheet
1 package of Rit of other commercial dye in a strong color such as red, blue, or purple, or 2 colors; paler shades for black babies
several large rubber bands.

Instructions

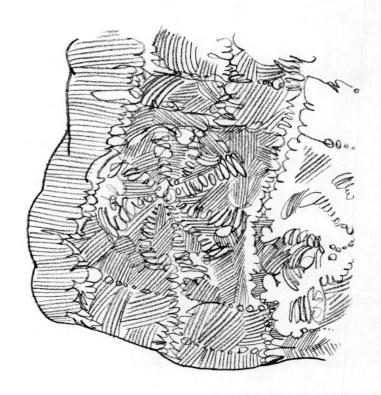

1. Gather up handfuls of the sheet here and there (a) and wind a rubber band around each handful many times as tightly as possible (b). (This process makes sunburst designs.)
2. Holding your hands at the sides of the sheet about 12″ from one end, gather the material in folds toward the center. Wrap tightly a large rubber band several times around the sheet where you wadded it (c). Gather again and wrap another band at a spot toward the other end of the sheet. Then gather and wrap bands at a couple of other spots between these 2 places. (This process makes stripes. The rubber bands hold the sheet in tight gathers which the dye can't penetrate. The white will remain in those gathers for color contrast with the dyed sections.)
3. Now follow instructions on package for dying. Rinse very thoroughly, until rinse water runs clear.

4. One strong color contrasting with the white background makes a fine sheet. If you wish more than 1 color, repeat the whole process after rinsing well. Always start with the lighter color and end with the darker.

How to Use

Use sheet in your baby's crib instead of solid white or pastel sheet. It will not lose color through machine washing.

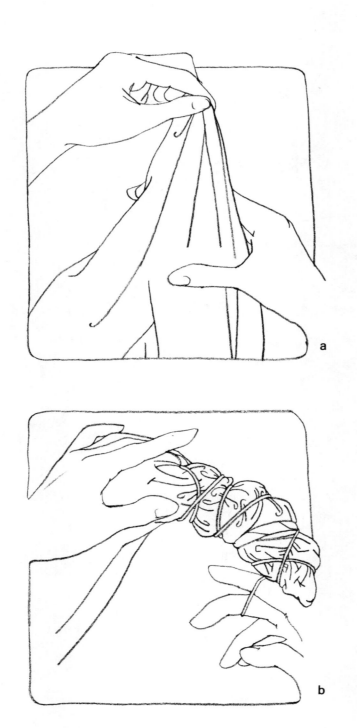

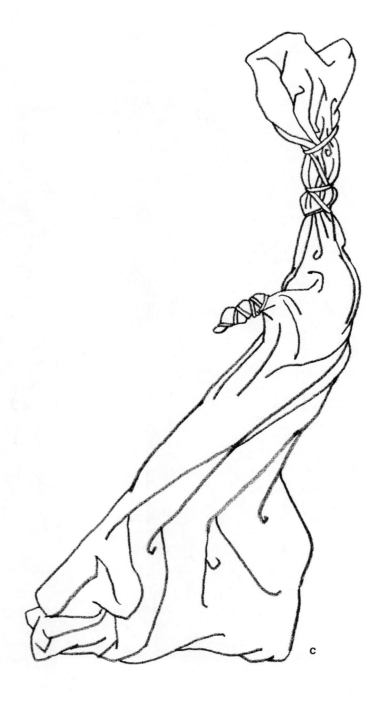

Birth to 1½ Months: Learning Comes from Looking

Chapter Two

1½ to 3½ Months: Hands Get into the Act

Education

Education begins in earnest now that your baby is accustomed to the real world outside the womb. Two dramatic signs that he is learning are his delectable smile and his discovery of his hands as moving objects worth watching. Now that he is starting to touch the things that he sees, he gets a lot more information about his new world.

Intelligence is the result of an interplay between heredity and environment. A carefully designed bassinet and crib environment can speed up and enhance mental development. Certain kinds of toys, strategically placed, invite the use of a baby's visual and manual skills. This use fosters the growth of intelligence.

To be stimulating an environment has to change as a baby's abilities advance. The parent or caregiver who designs the physical environment has to select the type of toy that best matches the baby's current style of interaction with objects. For instance, a baby who swipes imprecisely at an object should have a broad toy that swings to and fro. A baby who is ready to hold an object should have a stationary toy that doesn't swing. A cooing, active, alert, and smiling baby indicates that you have matched the toy to the ability level.

Every baby is innately curious. This curiosity can be fed by varying the things that he sees and feels. Variety is the spice of even a tiny infant's life.

At this stage physical and intellectual growth are closely connected. Vision improves, and the baby learns by perceiving more accurately. The coordination of hand movements begins, and the baby learns by locating objects in space with his hand, batting, feeling, and bringing them to his mouth. The more he practices focusing on and manipulating objects, the more these skills impact cognitive development.

Think about moving your child to a crib as soon as possible during this phase since it is a far more convenient piece of equipment than a bassinet in which to arrange educational toys. You might place your baby in a crib just for certain hours of the day. Bassinet sides are shallow and do not always permit the suspension of toys where they can be easily seen or touched. There's more room for toys in a crib. Also, crib mattresses can be moved up or down, allowing you to place the baby in the best position in relation to the toy. (See Dowel for Crib Toys, the first pattern in this chapter.)

BEHAVIORS

Visual examination of the details of toys continues throughout this stage. Keep varying your baby's "diet" with new sights. Although your baby may still turn her head toward the right when lying on her back, she is not looking to the far right now (near the mattress) but facing upwards toward the top of the bassinet or crib side. Soon she'll be centering her head and looking straight up. As her head position changes, you must gradually adjust the crib toys so they are always in her line of sight.

A baby touching a toy or studying her hand may wear an expression of intense concentration. Learning about her world is a serious business. But at about 2 months of age those delightful first smiles begin to flicker on her lips while she looks at you. Smiles also start appearing in response to a familiar toy

brought into view. By 2½ months she may smile repeatedly at a picture of a face or at a part of her mobile.

Fists are no longer always clenched. You can lay a toy in an open palm. Your baby will probably bring it to her mouth for gumming. Mouthing a toy is another important way for her to explore the feel of things.

Around 3 months she brings her hands together over her tummy and her fingers interweave with each other. If you place a toy in one hand, she brings it to this midline position and the other hand joins in for exploratory fingering.

A baby can now link together 2 actions that were previously performed separately. This linking is a sign of learning. The object she looks at, she now touches. The thing she holds, she now sucks. The sound she hears, she now turns toward to discover its source.

These behaviors clue you in to appropriate play. Hang a textured object over her hand and let her feel it. Give her a lightweight rattle that fits her little hand and she will gum it. Make a sound in a corner of the room and watch her turn toward you.

ABILITIES

A baby is now much more adept at tracking a big colorful object moved across his line of vision. He'll follow it many times in a row, fascinated. You can continue to use the Flying Saucer which you made for the first phase of development.

A baby can now focus on a 3-dimensional object as it gradually approaches his face from a few feet away. His focusing ability has become more flexible than in the first month. But the ideal position for graphics and objects you might show him is 8 to 12 inches from his eyes.

Mobiles made for the early weeks will continue to serve their purpose until your baby is 8 or 9 weeks old. When your baby starts touching, you should move them out of reach because they are fragile. You may hoist them as far as a yard away because your baby can now see things well enough at that distance. In the up-close position you can now place the batting toys described in this chapter.

Your baby wants to touch what he sees. However, he's not yet physically coordinated enough to reach for a toy and grasp it. Instead his desire to touch appears as an awkward swipe through the air. Sometimes the swipe makes contact, especially if the object is broad enough. Then if the object swings or rattles invitingly, he is encouraged to try hitting it again. This hitting is called "batting" by infant researchers. He hits toys with increasing precision and is soon batting "homers." For this purpose we have designed the Tambourine, Batting Practice, Easter Egg Hunt, and Tinkling Chimes.

If you don't want him to "strike out," dangle these toys in the proximity of those waving hands. They are all designed to be wide enough in diameter so that he can't miss. Place batting toys not only in his bed, but also in the carriage and in that area above the kitchen counter where he reclines in his infant seat. Let him have a wonderful time batting away to his heart's content.

Babies developing quickly may start batting before 2½ months, but many babies continue to examine just visually until another couple of weeks go by. After babies have been batting consistently for a few weeks, they will want to start catching hold of a toy. Then you should put away the batting toys and provide your baby with the Feelie Stabile described in Chapter Three. The semirigid arms hold objects in place rather than allowing them to swing away as the flexible string or yarn does. If your baby is developing quickly and batted early, he may start reaching and grasping early. In this case, he may be ready for the change to the Feelie Stabile at 3 months. Get it made in time.

INTERESTS

You can count on anything within 2 to 3 feet of your baby's eyes as being of interest and subject to intense perusal. Your baby still likes to stare at faces and pictures of faces, and will smile spontaneously seconds after being shown them. You can draw them with more complicated detail now or use large photographs from magazines.

Your baby will pay attention to 3-dimensional objects brought near her face and will glance from one point to another along their surfaces. We have designed a stuffed-animal mobile as one way to satisfy this interest (Menagerie Merry-Go-Round). You can find and present other 3-dimensional forms that are increasingly detailed and complex.

A desire to finger the surfaces of things is evolving at this time too. The satin edge of your baby's blanket may be the first object of such an urge. Our Fabric Sampler will also tempt your baby to begin some investigatory fingering.

Hand-watching may become a favorite pastime during this stage. The hand is a better toy than most inanimate objects for 2 reasons: It is always moving, and it is constantly changing its appearance. The fingers open and close, spread apart or touch each other, curl and straighten. These 2 characteristics, movement and variety, make the hand a superior plaything.

Although a hand "accidentally" disappears from view when the baby lowers her hand, it's bound to reappear; after all, it's attached! This gives the hand a distinct advantage over toys such as rattles which roll to the edge of the bassinet or under the blanket. The unpredictable disappearance and surprise reappearance of the hand also adds to its attractiveness. Merry Mitts, found in this chapter, will enable your baby to discover more readily and enjoy more keenly her hand movements.

10. Dowel for Crib Toys

Reason for Toy

This is not a toy but a cheap and convenient device for supporting toys over a baby's eyes and hands when the baby is in his crib or playpen. This is your basic piece of equipment for creating an interesting crib environment.

Materials

wooden dowel (from hardware store or lumber yard), about 36" long, ⅝" in diameter (see Variations if you are delayed in getting to the store to buy dowel)
heavyweight string
small rubber bands

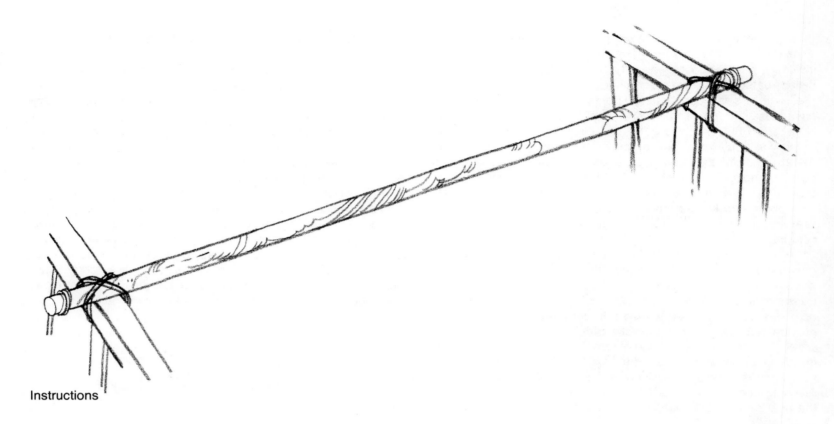

Instructions

1. With string, lash dowel securely to crib rails. You can wrap string around one of the vertical posts as well as the rail.
2. To keep dowel from slipping out of place when tied, wind a rubber band tightly around each end of dowel.

How to Use

Adjust mattress to lowest position. This level gives baby best view of hanging toys and best angle for practicing reaching and grasping. Toys meant to dangle over baby's hands may be suspended from dowel by string or yarn tied around dowel.

Toys should hang down from dowel to be within easy reach of baby's hands. Lowering mattress will probably facilitate baby's seeing of and reaching for toys, but you will have to bend over further when laying down or picking up your baby.

Smart Toys

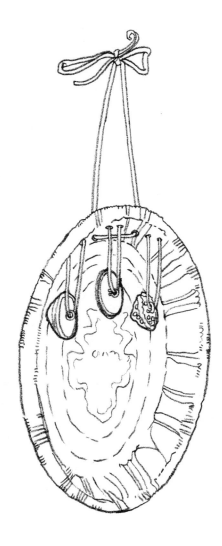

An old leather belt will substitute nicely for the wooden dowel. With string, lash buckle to crib rail and a post on one crib side. Thread string through one of holes at other end of belt and tie it around crib rail and a post on the other side. Punch some extra holes in belt through which you can thread yarn that is to hold a hanging object.

You can also stretch a man's tie across crib and knot it on each railing. This is fine for batting and the early days of reaching and grasping, but it will not be as strong as the dowel or belt when baby starts to pull.

A shock cord or tie-down with rubber covered hooks on each end also works nicely. These are available at bicycle or camping stores.

11. Tambourine

Reason for Toy

After 6 weeks, your baby begins to use her hands to explore. Not only does she look hard at a dangling toy but she raises her fist and takes a swipe at it. At first, contact seems to be by chance but soon it appears to occur on purpose. When the baby is rewarded with an interesting sound like a tiny clatter, she has greater incentive to try striking the object. Before long, your percussionist becomes quite accurate in her batting efforts.

Materials

9″ foil pie pan
3 metal buttons (brass or silver coat buttons), with loops on back
bright yarn, possibly of different colors

Instructions

1. Punch 3 pairs of close-together small holes along rim of pie pan, leaving 2″ between pairs.
2. Thread about a 5″-piece of yarn through loops on backs of buttons.
3. Hang a button by yarn through each pair of holes and tie tightly on outside of pie pan. Buttons should hang down about 2″ inside pan rim.
4. Below holes for the middle button, punch 2 more holes 2″ apart.
5. Put 2′-length of yarn through these holes and tie the ends in a double knot and bow to form a hanging cord. Suspend pan with buttons on top, hanging down into pan.

How to Use

Tie tambourine onto dowel. Hang near enough to baby's right or left hand so that when she waves it, she'll come in contact with the tambourine. When she learns to bat the pie pan consistently on purpose and starts to become bored with toy, hang tambourine above her toes. She'll soon realize she can make it jingle-jangle by kicking instead of arm-waving.

Safety Note

When you have finished this toy, make sure buttons are securely fastened and will not fall off. Baby should tap lower part of pie pan and not touch buttons. Care must be taken with any construction suspended over a baby so that nothing will come loose and be ingested. Don't let an older sibling mishandle this toy.

Smart Toys

12. Batting Practice

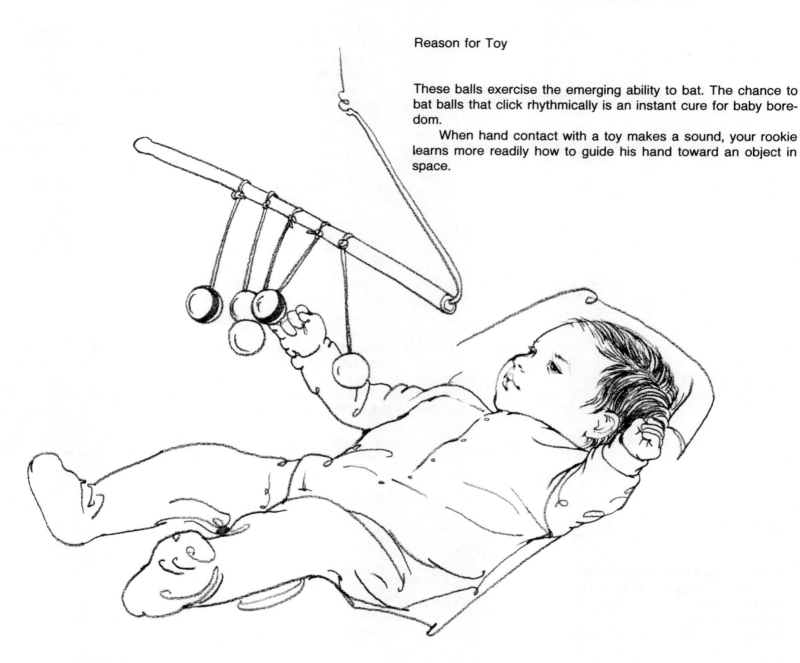

These balls exercise the emerging ability to bat. The chance to bat balls that click rhythmically is an instant cure for baby boredom.

When hand contact with a toy makes a sound, your rookie learns more readily how to guide his hand toward an object in space.

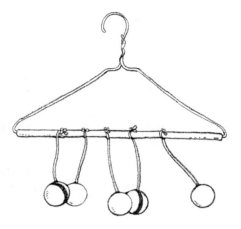

Instructions

1. With razor blade or mat knife, cut a tiny slit in each ball.
2. Cut 5 lengths of string 7″ to 8″ long. Tie a couple of knots at the end of each.
3. Poke the knotted end of each string through the slit in a ball. See that the slit closes firmly and knotted end doesn't slip out (a).
4. Cut cloth tape ¼″ wide and wrap around 2 balls so stripe shows from beneath (a).
5. For extra good looks, wrap strip of cloth tape or Con-Tact paper around the cardboard hanger roll.
6. Cut grooves in the cardboard roll 1″ to 1¾″ apart. Tie each string in a groove.

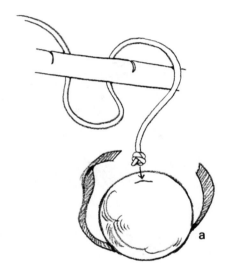

a

How to Use

Hang toy near open window or outdoors where breeze will make the balls tap each other. Look for hooks, bars, knobs, or cabinet doors on which to hang the hanger.

Always place balls within touching range of your baby's fingers. Perhaps he lies in his infant seat on the floor a lot; then tie each end of a string to a stationary object such as a piece of furniture, letting the string sag in the middle as low as is necessary to allow balls to be near hands when hanger is hooked over string.

Materials

5 white or yellow Ping-Pong balls
wire clothes hanger with cardboard roll
black cloth tape
lightweight string
cloth tape or Con-Tact paper

Variation

At 3½ months, position balls so that they dangle over your baby's kicking feet.

13. Easter Egg Hunt

Reason for Toy

Finding with her hand the object your baby sees is a real hunt at this age. Contact may happen by accident at first, then a more purposeful but crude swipe in space develops, often missing the mark. However, the pleasure of hearing a rattle improves the aim quickly.

Materials

3 plastic Easter eggs designed to hold candy, or L'eggs pantyhose
   cases
dried beans, pebbles, buttons
lightweight string
epoxy

Instructions

1. Measure the distance from the dowel across bassinet or crib to the area of your baby's hands. Cut 3 lengths of string accordingly, allowing a few extra inches for tying around the dowel.

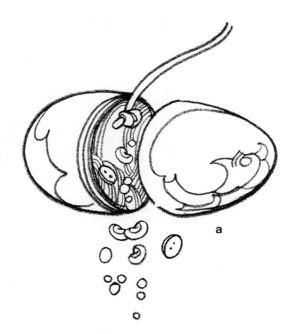

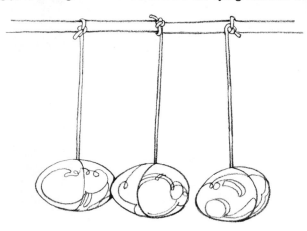

2. Tie a knot in the end of each string.
3. Put a few beans and/or pebbles or a button inside one half of each egg (a).
4. Epoxy the rims of the egg halves. Just before pressing them together, slip the knot inside the whole egg (a).
5. Let epoxy dry overnight.

How to Use

Tie each string on bassinet holder or crib dowel. Eggs should touch each other when dangling. Run your finger along them occasionally as you pass by so they bump each other.

Safety Note

Test eggs every day or so to make sure glue has not loosened. You do not want the bits inside to fall out because a baby could gag on such small items.

14. Tinkling Chimes

Reason for Toy

These chimes reward the baby's first efforts to use his hands. When he strikes with fisted or unfisted hand, he hears a pleasant tinkle. This creates a desire to strike again. Gradually, accuracy develops.

Materials

3 empty long metal containers, the type used for individual cigars
3 ribbons, fabric scraps, or strings
epoxy

Instructions

1. With ice pick or knife point, punch a hole in each lid, from the outside toward the inside (so rough edges will be inside).
2. If using fabric scraps to suspend chimes, cut 3 strips ½" wide with pinking shears. The length of the scraps, strings, or ribbons should be about 20".
3. With ice pick or knife point, poke the ribbon through the hole in each lid. Inside, tie several tight knots in the ribbon to keep it from coming back out the hole (a).
4. Glue lids to containers with epoxy and let glue dry overnight.

How to Use

Tie ribbons to dowel across crib, hanging chimes about 1" apart. Make sure they dangle over the right or left hand so a casual swipe through the air will be likely to make contact with them.

Variation

To use this toy in kitchen, family room, or backyard, tie ribbons to a string. Stretch string over baby in infant seat by tying one end to a doorknob or other stationary object and holding the other end. A sibling can enjoy watching for the baby's reactions. (See illustration on page 18.)

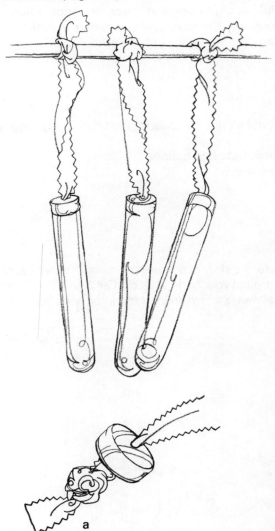

a

15. Merry Mitts*

Reason for Toy

A baby begins to stare at her own hands sometime after 2 months. She holds one up before her face about 5 to 6 inches from her eyes. Watching the "dance" of her individual fingers is quite intriguing. A pair of colorful mitts will help your baby find her hands sooner than nature would allow, as the bright pattern will flag down her attention earlier than plain skin would.

The advantage of early discovery of the hands is that such absorbed watching can soothe the restlessness of a young baby unable to do much else for fun. Hands provide a stage show, and she may spend many hours during her third month spectating.

Materials

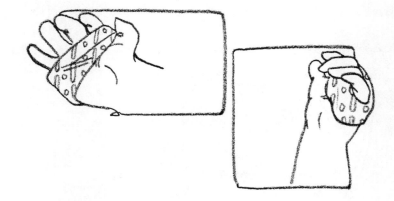

small piece of fabric, a stretchy one if possible, with tiny figured pattern or narrow stripes, cut with pinking shears
thread

Instructions

1. Cut 2 short strips of fabric about 1½" wide and long enough to just fit the circumference of your baby's palm, allowing a bit extra for a seam.
2. Make a seam where the ends meet to form circular bands.

How to Use

When your baby is in a cheerful mood, slip these mitts on over the fingers, excluding the thumb. They fit a bit like golf gloves. Later, when steady staring at a hand has begun, the mitts, used occasionally, serve to vary the appearance of the hands.

---

* Design concept originated by Burton L. White

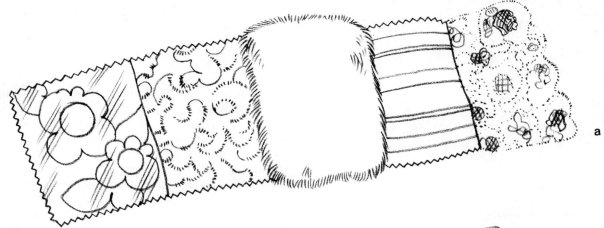

16. Fabric Sampler

Reason for Toy

Babies get pleasure from using their fingers for the simple act of stroking the surfaces of things. Here you offer your baby a variety of fingertip sensations.

Materials

swatches of 5 very different fabrics such as lace, fake fur (a favorite), polished cotton, oilcloth, terrycloth, brocade, stretchy fabric, plain cotton, cut velvet, vinyl
thread

Instructions

1. With pinking shears cut rectangles from 5 different fabrics, each rectangle about 4″ x 5″.
2. Sew them together in a line, making a seam between neighboring swatches (a).

Tack with thread the corners of sampler to the bassinet holder. Sampler should hang within touching distance of hands. Or hand-sew the train of fabrics in a ring around the safety belt across car seat or stroller. Little fingers can fidget for fun during boring car pools or on department store rounds.

17. Menagerie Merry-Go-Round

Reason for Toy

This mobile of stuffed animals puts to good use those furry gifts your new baby probably received. Ears, noses, and paws protruding from torsos invite your baby to tug and yank, thus encouraging early reach-and-grasp instincts.

Materials

1 metal or wood ring, 8″ or more in diameter (could be macramé ring from crafts store)
several small stuffed animals (those shown are 6″ to 8″ tall)
heavyweight string or strong yarn
yarn for decorating ring (optional)

Instructions

1. Wrap yarn around ring if you wish to add color. (See instructions for Jingle Bells in Chapter Three.)
2. Take a 20″-piece of string or strong yarn. Tie center of it on ring (a). Now tie both ends securely to other side of ring. Tie another string at right angles to the first (b).
3. At the center where they meet, tie on another piece of string to form loop for hanging (c).

4. Loop the center of a length of string around neck or stomach of each animal and knot it at the back of the neck or on the back. Make sure animals will hang facing down toward baby.
5. Now loop the string around the ring. Tie, leaving ends long enough to tie again (d). Holding the ring in mid-air, slide the animals around on it until it balances. When it does, tie the ends of each string around ring to keep each animal anchored in its proper position.

How to Use

Tie Merry-Go-Round to dowel on crib or move dowel to playpen and tie there.

18. Playtime Floor Mat

Reason for Toy

Have baby, will travel! Whether you take your baby to the office, his grandmother's house, or a friend's apartment, this floor mat provides a soft, clean spot to deposit him while you work or chat. At home the mat offers your offspring a view of the world different from the one he gets when inside the bassinet. It provides a location for spreading out his toys once he can lie on his tummy, head held up, and examine them.

Materials

2 pieces of fabric, 36" x 45" (colorfast and preferably permanent press), one piece a solid color, the other a figured print (see Variation below and, if you prefer, use 2 solid pieces)
1 piece of polyester quilt filling, 36" x 45"
1 ribbon, 36" long
thread

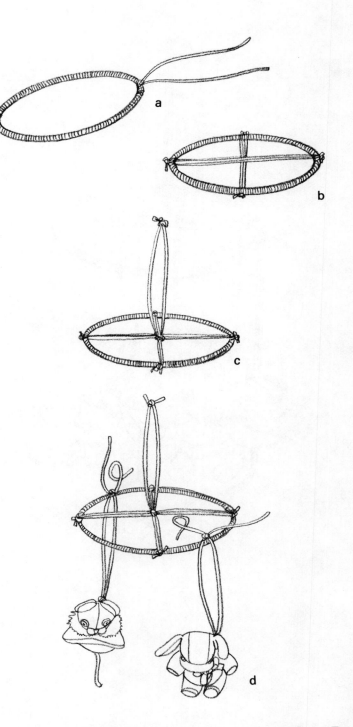

Instructions

1. Lay out the 2 pieces of fabric, right sides together, and lay polyester quilt filling on top.
2. Sew all around ½″ from edge, leaving a 10″ opening on one side.
3. Turn right-side out and hand-stitch opening closed.
4. Top-stitch all around ½″ from edge.
5. Securely sew the center of your ribbon to the edge of the mat on the plain side at a spot about 9″ from the corner of the 36″ side of your mat.

How to Use

Place mat in kitchen, laundry room, or on sun deck—wherever you are. Roll up, tie, and stuff in a tote bag when you leave home (a).

The plain side of the mat makes a good background for toys, as the colors and the graphics on the toys show up well.

Variation

You can use a solid fabric for both sides and appliqué your own design on one side. The appliqué work should be done first, before step 1. The model mat illustrated is red with 3 butterflies.

To make, cut out 2 large wings from one tiny patterned fabric and 2 small wings from another print. Pin the butterflies in place and zigzag-stitch around them on a sewing machine, using a different brightly colored thread for each butterfly. Pencil a line for the body and feelers and zigzag-stitch over it. Now go on to step 1 above.

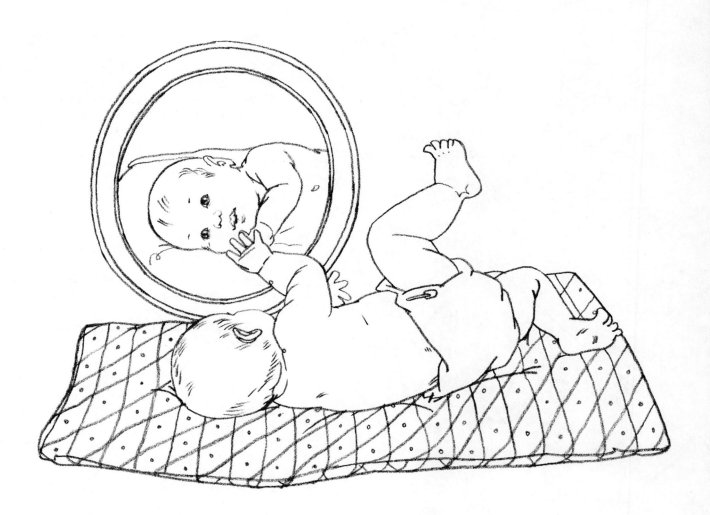

Chapter Three

3½ to 5½ Months: Reach-and-Grasp Experiences

EDUCATION

A baby shouldn't have to while away her awake time in an uninvolved way. Educating your baby at this stage consists of making sure she spends part of every day in a place where she can have the kind of experiences that give her pleasure and sometimes excitement. This means designing the crib or playpen environment to include reachable objects which are interestingly shaped and textured.

It may mean suspending toys on a support device in the back of the station wagon, if your baby spends a lot of time there while you are driving. Or you may jerry-build a holder for toys just in front of the place where you put her in her infant seat indoors or outdoors.

Your baby is on her way to becoming an intelligent being. The problem-solving abilities which she will possess as a toddler have their origin in this period. From now until 6 months of age your baby will be working on her ability to reach out and grasp a toy within arm's length. The final mastery of this hand movement, which occurs under the guidance of her eyes, is called "visually directed reaching" by educational researchers. This is considered a landmark in cognitive development.

It's unlikely that most parents realize what a taste for variety infants have and what a capacity they have to take in new sights! This characteristic is not to be interpreted simply as a short attention span, but rather as an appreciation for the novel and a lively curiosity. So nourish that zest for life!

The objects you keep for awhile in the crib can be moved to the car or altered slightly in appearance and thus become "new" toys. Altering can simply consist of adding a decorative note to a toy (for example, wrapping around it a strip of colored tape) or subtracting a component part from it (unscrewing the lid).

Just as you long for your own day to be interesting and plan it accordingly, so you should also want your baby's day to be interesting for her. If you make and present the toys from the patterns which follow, there is little chance your baby will get bored. And a baby who is pleased and content keeps on learning.

BEHAVIORS

Life is definitely a bowl of cherries at this age. Babies smile a lot and begin to laugh. Their sunny mood can last all day long. They are sociable with relatives, baby-sitters, and workers at the day-care center. Plan on being nearby to enjoy as many moments as possible of this idyllic time.

Skip household chores when you can and play with this genial creature. Talk to your baby, smile at him, express affection. But you don't really need to be told this because babies have a way, at this age, of irresistibly attracting their parents' involvement. And if you reward happy looks and gurgles with attention, this reinforces an infant's awareness that one of the best ways to get attention is to be charming. Give him many opportunities when he can be with you and, simultaneously, have a good time. This begins cementing the close relationship to which you aspire.

ABILITIES

A 4-month-old is a sharp observer. She thoroughly scrutinizes the objects hung over her head or given her. You have a student in the nursery who studies the textures, shapes, sizes, colors, and contours of inanimate objects. She can now track targets moving in circles or along diagonals. Her vision is as good as that of a young adult.

She continues to watch her hands, learning how to make use of them as reaching tools. She constantly exercises the ability to grasp a nearby plaything. She watches her hands carefully as they move toward and try to catch hold of an object. There appears to be a built-in drive urging her toward the mastery of this skill of reaching and grasping.

The process of mastering the skill is not simple. First, an infant has to locate the object with her eyes. Next, she must move her hand out in precisely the right direction of the object. Then just before contact, she must open her fingers or close them slightly to prepare them for grasping. Finally, she grasps.

During this phase, which can begin as early as 3 months, put away the batting toys which dangle from strings. A baby's first clumsy efforts at reaching for and grasping these will cause them to swing away from her hand and she'll feel frustrated. Instead, now attach objects to semirigid holding arms like those in our dowel-and-hanger device called Feelie Stabile. A pattern for it is included in this chapter. Then the objects will stay in that corner of space where the baby has spotted them and toward which she is coordinating her hand movements. Once she has grasped an object, she may release it, then reach for and hold it again. She may try various investigatory finger movements on it—poking, rubbing, twisting, or wobbling the object.

Now noticeable is another distinct step of development regarding the hands. Until the fourth month your baby keeps her hands apart, using them independently. Now when she's lying on her back, she brings them together over her tummy, interlacing her fingers. Baby-watchers have called this phenomenon "hands-to-midline clasping." You can place a toy in one of your baby's hands and she'll bring the other hand over to join in feeling the toy. She'll probably stare hard at it, perhaps turn it around to see how it looks at different angles. She may transfer it back and forth from one hand to the other. We include several clutch toys on the following pages for this activity.

Other new abilities of this age are sturdy kicking and rolling over from tummy to back and vice versa. When your baby feels something like the footboard of her crib against the soles of her feet, she likes to thrust out her legs. A strong kick toy to push against will please the budding soccer player. Patterns follow for two such toys. When she starts rolling over onto her tummy, you can have ready for examination a few toys arranged on a floor mat, in addition to the toys that have been positioned overhead.

INTERESTS

Your baby's main interests are still confined to the people and things that appear within 3 feet of his eyes. He's relatively indifferent to what's across the room or out the window. To guarantee variety in his immediate surroundings, change his location in the house throughout the day. Propped up in his infant seat in the kitchen, lying on a floor mat in the living room, or being outdoors in a playpen are situations that offer him a change of scenery. Make sure that in each setting you place him near some furnishings or objects of interest; for example, put him near colorful mixing bowls in the kitchen or patterned drapes in the living room, flowers or shrubs in the yard.

Any day now he will also catch sight of his kicking feet and watch them. He will finger his little toes and put his feet in his wet mouth.

Your baby still watches the movements of his fingers, but now he is more intent on how his hand works as a tool for him—feeling surface textures and grasping objects. He loves to check out how these things feel in his hands and in his mouth. Are they hard or soft, rough or smooth, spongy or stiff? He also wants to bat and grab them. He is delighted if they jiggle, wobble, rattle, or ring when he makes contact.

You can use your own imagination and resources when attaching objects to our Feelie Stabile; you do not have to use only those pictured. Your infant will appreciate any small, safe, interestingly contoured, and colorful objects you would like to substitute to give him a new and different feeling experience.

As your baby perfects his reach and grasp, however, he outgrows his need for the semirigid arms of the Feelie Stabile. He can now catch hold of a handle that is dangling on a string. Two of our toys—Jingle Bells and Bell Ringer—have handles that, once yanked, produce jingling and clanking sounds that reward your baby for his efforts. His ability to make things happen to objects gives him the impression that he is a Very Important Person.

Your baby will enjoy an unbreakable mirror placed in his bed, playpen, or at eye level beside the changing table. Flirting with his image will keep him entranced for quite a few minutes.

SAFETY NOTE

All toys and household utensils should now be mouthable: nontoxic, colorfast, and without sharp points or rough edges. Check that they have no small parts that could fall off or be pulled off.

19. Wrist and Ankle Bracelets

Reason for Toy

If your baby has not yet noticed her hand, these bracelets may capture her attention and lead her to focus on her hand. If she does watch her hand, these ornaments will add an extra attraction to the view. When your baby wears the bell bracelet, her frequent hand-waving will produce a jingle. This sound will be especially amusing if she's alone in a silent room.

The bell bracelet worn on an ankle can cause little feet that have been fairly stationary to start kicking to beat the band! At the beginning of this stage a baby can't really see her feet; toward the end, a baby discovers her feet and starts playing with them. Either pair of bracelets hastens the pleasant discovery of hands and feet, those "built-in" playthings.

Materials

dress elastic, ¼" or ⅜" wide
brass or silver coat button with loop on back or a bead
sleigh bell
heavy cardboard
thread
small ball of yarn

Instructions

Bell and Button Bracelets for Wrist:

1. Cut dress elastic to just fit around baby's wrist with a little overlap.
2. Sew it securely together in a ring.
3. Make another bracelet for the other hand.
4. Thread a bit of yarn through back of button or bead and tie it onto one elastic bracelet. Thread another bit of yarn through back of sleigh bell and tie it to other bracelet (a).

Pompon Bracelets for Ankle:

1. Make 2 rings of elastic as described in other bracelet pattern.
2. To make yarn pompon, cut a strip of heavy cardboard 1½" wide. Wrap around it a brightly colored yarn 50 times (b). Slip the wrapped yarn off cardboard and tie it tightly around the middle with another piece of yarn about 9" long. Leave the ends of the 9"-piece long for tying the pompon onto elastic (c). Now make another pompon for the other ring of elastic.
3. Give the pompons a "haircut" so fringe is even and fluff out so they are round and pretty.
4. Tie each pompon to a bracelet.

How to Use

Move the bell and button pair of bracelets from wrists to feet after a couple of weeks. These can be worn around feet or ankles.

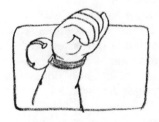

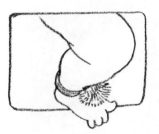

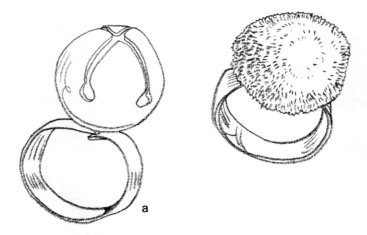

They may be seen better when around feet, but they may fall off or be pulled off. If such is the case, try the ankles.

Change the pompon bracelets from feet to hands or wrists. A switch like this is always stimulating for a baby. Arms and legs will wave excitedly in response to the change.

Safety Note

Keep checking button or bead, bell, and pompons to make sure they are securely fastened. They are small enough to be swallowed if detached. Beware they are not being chewed off.

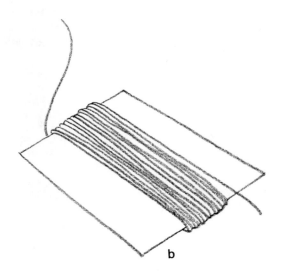

20. Feelie Stabile

Reason for Toy

Babies enjoy investigating the textures of things. This "feelie" toy enables them to experience 3 different textures. Of course the variety in shape is pleasing too.

Because the support arms are semirigid the objects are in the same place every time a baby grabs for them. It is frustrating to a baby learning to reach if an object swings away as he touches it.

Materials

wire clothes hanger
lightweight string
brightly colored plastic or cloth tape, about 1″ wide
bottle brush (like a string mop)
rectangular sponge
plastic mesh pot scrubber or plastic-bristled scrubber on handle

Instructions

1. Bend wire hanger into 2 arms (a).
2. With string lash handle of bottle brush to center of hanger (b).
3. Punch 2 holes in the sponge, thread string through them, and tie onto end of one arm of hanger (c).
4. Put another piece of string through center of pot scrubber and tie it to the other arm (d).
5. Wrap tape around both wire arms of hanger, handle of bottle brush, and joint where handle is lashed to hanger. Leave wire ends of hanger arms free from tape so you can untie original objects and put on new ones occasionally.

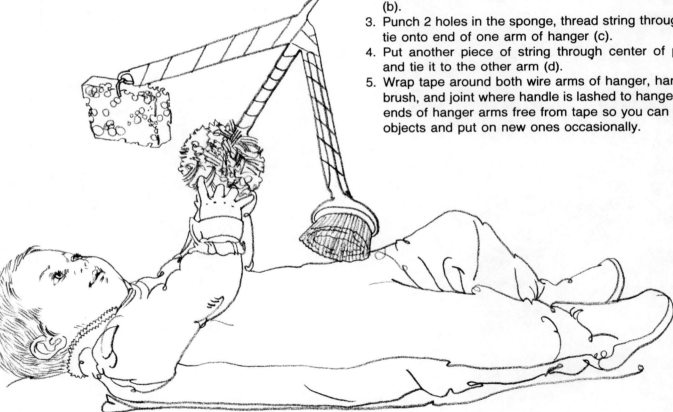

How to Use

To suspend Feelie Stabile securely over your baby, make 2 holes in your crib dowel about 2″ apart with a hand or electric drill. (See Dowel for Crib Toys, Chapter Two.) These holes should be slightly to the left or right of the center of the dowel. Insert hook of hanger into one hole from underneath. Then slide hook into other hole from above. This position makes your Stabile really stable (e).

Variations

This hanger device is not a single toy. It is a basic holder to which you should attach a variety of objects over the next 3 months. Remove original items as baby begins losing interest in them and substitute other safe household objects. (See Serendipity List at end of this book for ideas.) If a new utensil has a handle, tape it along the hanger arm.

For example, you could tie on one of the Easter eggs from the batting toy made during the previous phase (Chapter Two). Tie it right at the end of the hanger arm so it no longer dangles. You could tie on a cigar case from the Tinkling Chimes toy also. Tie it tightly to the wire without leaving any length of string for dangling; now its smooth metal can be felt.

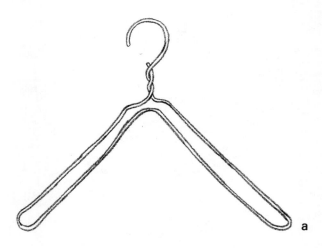

a

b

c

d

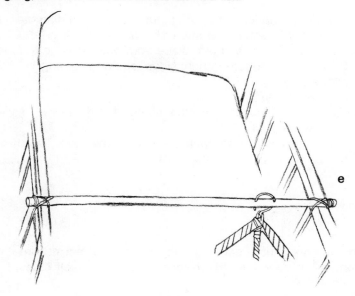

e

21. Doughnut Clutch Toy

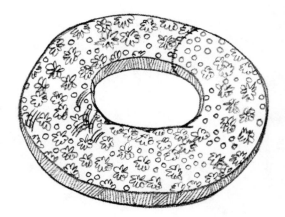

Reason for Toy

After your baby takes this toy with one hand, she may bring her other hand over to join in examination of it. Hands playing together over the tummy is a step of progress from the stage where hands were kept apart and used independently.

Materials

2 different bright, colorfast fabrics
polyester pillow filling or cotton or old nylon hose for stuffing
sleigh bell (optional)
thread

Instructions

1. From both fabrics cut a doughnut shape 7″ in diameter. The diameter of center hole should be about 1″.
2. Cut across shapes in one place from outside edge to center.
3. Sew 2 pieces together (right sides together) leaving ½″ seam allowance.
4. Clip seams (a).
5. Turn right side out and stuff tightly (b). If desired, stick in bell as you stuff.
6. Turn under edges at open ends and sew them together by hand.

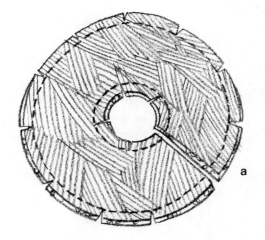

a

How to Use

Hold the doughnut near your baby's hand. Let her admire it and then, in her own time, reach for it. For play-by-self times, lay it on floor mat.

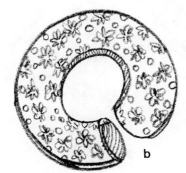

b

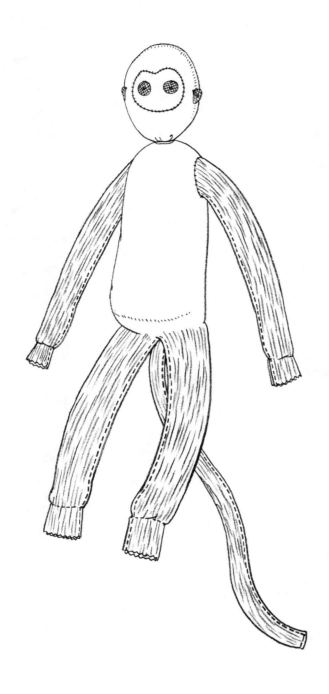

22. Sock Monkey*

Reason for Toy

Your baby enjoys taking in *his* hand a toy offered by *your* hand. This toy can be grasped conveniently by arm, leg, or tail. When released, the monkey tends to linger in a baby's lap (formed by the infant seat) rather than drop to the floor.

Materials

pair of men's knitted socks
polyester pillow filling
bits of black and white felt
thread

Instructions

1. Stuff toe of 1 sock to form head. Tie a thread several times around to make neck (a).
2. Holding sock with the heel part of sock turned toward you, cut leg of sock down the middle almost to heel (b).
3. Stuff body part down to slit (b).
4. Stitch sides together all around slit (c).
5. Stuff legs and sew across ends about 1″ from edge (c).
6. Cut off leg part of other sock. Cut it in half to make 2 arms.
7. Sew them lengthwise and across the end about 1″ from edge at one end.
8. Stuff and sew raw edges onto body.
9. Cut a piece of white felt for face and sew on 2 black circles for eyes (d).
10. Cut 2 little black felt ears and sew onto sides of head (d).
11. Cut all along edge of remaining sock foot, making a strip about ½″ wide. Hold it out straight and stitch it close to edge and across ends (e). Sew this on for a tail.

How to Use

With your baby lying on his back or sitting in infant seat, offer the toy to him. He will almost always reach forward and grasp for it.

* Design by Emily Sparks

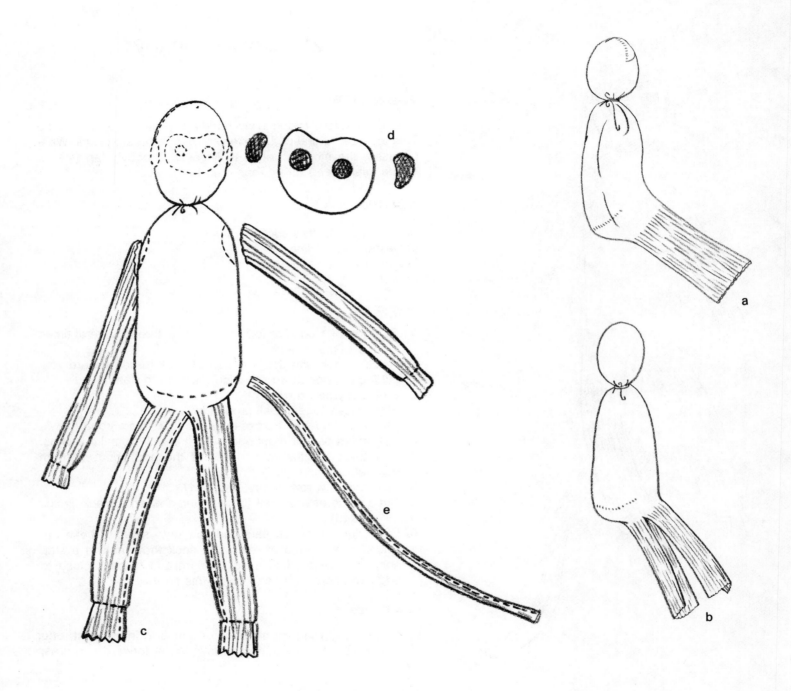

23. Spoon Friend

Reason for Toy

As fingers interweave over the tummy, your baby can now incorporate a toy in this 10-finger play. Here's a hard, solid object to clutch in contrast to the 2 previous soft ones. Reaching for and grasping it, feeling, and gumming it will produce a different set of sensations. Watch your baby watch her hands manipulating this spoon.

Materials

wooden spoon, 7" long (you can saw off handle if too long; be
  sure to sand the end)
piece of ribbon, 4" long
permanent-ink felt-tip pen

Instructions

1. Draw a happy face on front of spoon and a sad face on back.
2. Tie ribbon around handle for a bow tie.

How to Use

Keep this toy in your purse to whip out during tedious moments driving in the car or waiting in line somewhere. Your baby will now reach, usually with her right hand, for almost any object presented to her. She may hold it a short distance from her eyes, simply looking at it, or she may bring it to her mouth and gum it.

24. Bell-Ringer

Reason for Toy

Reaching and grasping is more fun when there's a sound feed-back. To the simple grasp, your baby now adds a pull. To the simple pull, she can add a to-and-fro swing. Every new way to use her hands under the guidance of her eyes furthers cognitive development.

Materials

empty tin can, about 4″ high, 2½″ in diameter
wooden bead, about ¾″ in diameter
wooden curtain ring (with screw eye), 2½″ in diameter
  (bead and ring available at hardware store)
brightly colored and patterned fabric scrap or ribbon

Instructions

1. Cut fabric scrap about 18″ long and ½″ wide with pinking shears.
2. Remove label and one end of can.
3. Punch hole in end of can with ice pick or knife point.
4. Poke the fabric scrap or ribbon through the hole. Draw it far through the can.
5. About 8″ up from the bottom end, tie a knot. (This anchors the lower section of the ribbon inside the can.)
6. String the bead onto the lower part of the ribbon up to the knot. Now tie another knot 2″ down from the first. (When you hold the top end of the ribbon taut, the bead should dangle level with the bottom half-inch of the can.)
7. Tie the lower end of the ribbon to screw eye on the curtain ring.
8. You could also tie a knot in ribbon just above the can so section of ribbon does not slide down through hole before you position it on crib dowel.

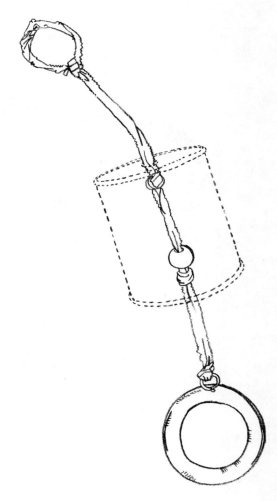

How to Use

Tie top part of ribbon to crib dowel over baby's right or left hand, or tie toy to hood of baby carriage. Next time your baby wakes up from a nap, she may "ring for you." "At your service, Miss!"

Safety Note

Although baby should not be able to reach can, its edges should be smooth in case an older child touches the toy.

25. Jingle Bells

Reason for Toy

This toy exercises your baby's use of his hand as a tool. Your infant is an activist who likes to make things happen. An accomplished reacher pulls on this handle and immediately makes the bells jiggle and jingle. He enjoys causing such an interesting effect.

Materials

8″-diameter metal or wooden macramé ring or embroidery hoop
strong brightly colored yarn, string, or thin ribbon
6 sleigh bells
wooden curtain ring (with screw eye), about 2″ in diameter
Elmer's Glue-All

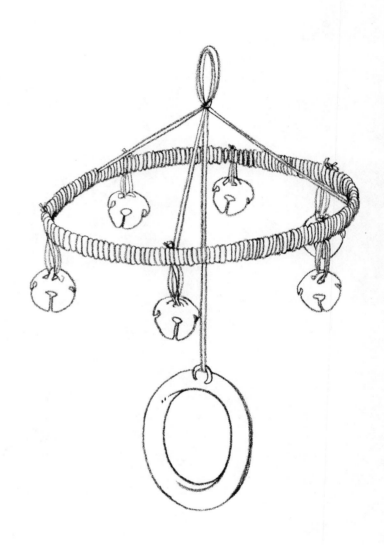

Instructions

1. Wrap the ring with yarn, completely covering it (a). Secure the ends with glue.
2. Tie on 6 bells, knotting the yarn on each bell, and knotting it twice, above and below the ring, so as to anchor each bell in one spot along the ring's circumference (b).
3. Space bells evenly around the ring and tie on 3 doubled lengths of yarn. Knot them where they come together in a centered position above the ring. Then make a loop at the ends for hanging.
4. Tie on to the lower knot another doubled length of yarn to dangle below the macramé ring as a bell pull.
5. Tie the end of this yarn to the screw eye of the curtain ring to make a handle for pulling. Suspend toy high enough so baby has to reach his arm up for handle and can't reach as far as the bells above.

How to Use

Slide loop onto dowel across playpen, or slip loop onto hanging plant hook. Be sure ring is close enough to your baby for him to grasp it. The length of hanging yarn may have to be adjusted according to distance between dowel or hook and baby's hands.

Safety Note

The baby is to pull on the handle *only* and not to touch or pull on the bells which, if pried off, are small enough to swallow. Hang it high enough so that the bells are out of reach. Continue to check that bells are tied on tightly.

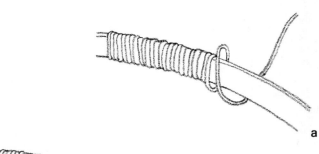

a

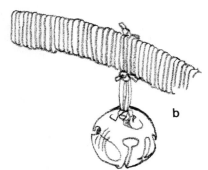

b

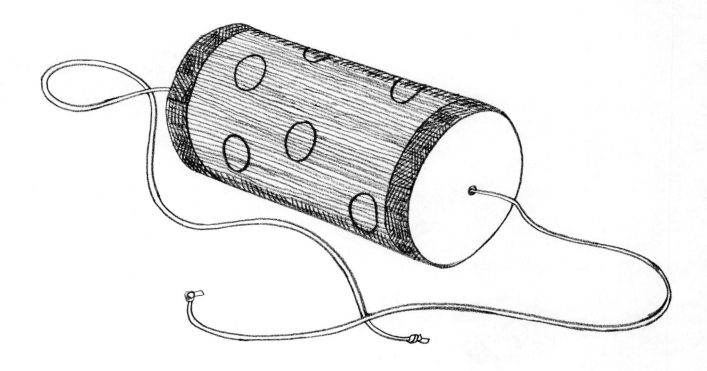

26. Field-Goal Kicker

Reason for Toy

While on her back your baby now starts holding her feet just above the mattress and, from a knees-bent position, thrusts her legs straight out. Kicking frequently over the next few months strengthens her legs for the day she pulls herself to a standing position.

The Field-Goal Kicker makes this early motor activity more enjoyable. Kicks produce a titillating clatter. This reinforces your baby's tendency to exercise her kicking skill often.

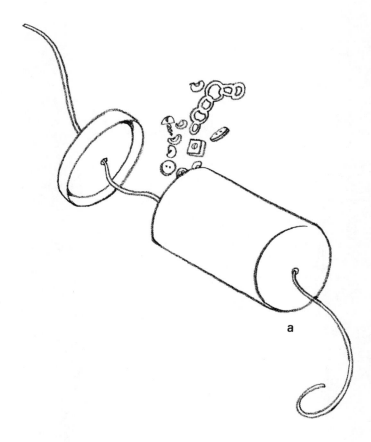

Materials

large cylindrical oatmeal box, about 9″ tall, 3″ in diameter
piece of fabric, possibly corduroy, 9½″ x 17½″
cloth tape
heavy string, cord, or ribbon, about 5′ long
Elmer's Glue-All
metal pieces from old jewelry or broken hardware, buttons, and
   paper clips, or dried beans

Instructions

1. Open box and put inside several items that make a noise
   when box is shaken; possibilities are listed under Materials.
2. Poke a small hole with scissors in bottom of box. Push string
   through hole and out through another hole punched in lid (a).
3. Glue lid on box.
4. Smear glue all over box and cover with piece of fabric.
5. Tape box around ends.

How to Use

Pulling string taut, tie ends to posts on each side of crib near
footboard. Dangle box an inch or more above mattress. Place
baby so her feet touch the toy.

Variation

For older baby, remove string and tape over holes. Let her roll
box around on floor.

27. Springy Kickboard

Reason for Toy

Foot-watching is a new pastime for your baby these days. The kickboard vibrating resiliently under rowdy thumping enables the feet to put on a good show for the eager spectator.

Materials

¼"-thick plywood, cut 13" x 15"
4 pieces of heavy waistband elastic, ¾" wide and 12" long
sandpaper
acrylic or other nontoxic paint

Instructions

1. Drill a hole in each corner of the plywood large enough to thread your elastic through.
2. Sand the wood and paint it a bright color. Paint on a simple design if you like.
3. Thread an elastic through each corner hole and knot it securely (a).

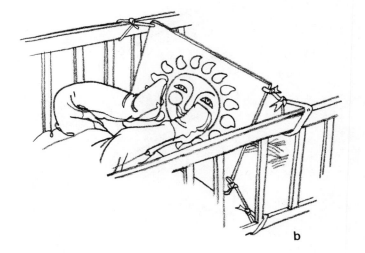

How to Use

Suspend kickboard 6" from the foot of the bed by tying the elastic straps to the sides of the crib. Tie the top elastic to the crib rail and the bottom elastic to a post below, near the mattress (b). Pull the elastic quite tight when you fasten it. The kickboard will still be springy enough to satisfy a bantam kicker.

a

Chapter Four

5½ to 8 Months: Experimenting with Cause and Effect

EDUCATION

The experiences your baby has during this phase form the foundations of his intelligence. You are the architect supervising the laying of these foundations. Of course your baby's natural curiosity guarantees much progress in the development of his mind. He will continue to investigate visually and explore manually without any urging from you. Nevertheless, by becoming very aware of your baby's current abilities and interests, you can enhance the quality of his daily experiences.

Through careful planning and thoughtful presentation of materials you can set up some learning opportunities that will ensure that the foundations of intelligence are laid more deeply, broadly, and securely than if you left the process to chance. A blueprint to use in managing your infant's daily experiences would include the following elements: the time to play with small objects, the chance to work simple mechanisms, and the opportunity to solve extremely simple problems. It is also essential that your baby hear you talk a lot about what he is seeing, hearing, and touching. At the end of this phase, he will indicate that he understands the meaning of several words, such as *Mommy, Daddy, baby, bye-bye, shoe,* and *ball.*

Each of these activities fosters a particular aspect of mental growth. As your baby plays with small objects—dropping, throwing, and banging them—he begins to perceive that he can be the *cause* of an interesting effect. ("I shake the can; it rattles.") He can make things happen. This leads him to study the *result* of his actions on objects. Thus a perception of the relationship of cause to effect is born. What an important building block in cognitive development!

The chance to operate simple mechanisms lets curious babies see how things work. They love to pull the plug and watch a sink drain, push a button and see the TV screen light up, press a lever and hear the vacuum cleaner roar.

Sometime between 6 and 8 months of age, babies solve their first problem in life. That first primitive problem is the same for every baby: an obstacle stands between him and a toy he wants. One day something clicks, and he pushes aside the obstacle to get the toy.

You can have fun setting up some very simple problems for your baby by putting an easy-to-remove obstacle in front of a favorite toy. His pushing aside the obstacle and grasping the toy will create a moment of small triumph, and such small triumphs are good for babies. The game of peek-a-boo is a similar problem situation. An obstacle, such as a pair of hands or a diaper, is hiding Mom's or Dad's face. When the obstacle is removed, the problem is solved and your baby feels gleeful. A baby readily learns to yank away the diaper covering a face.

Hide-and-seek games are also problem-solving situations. As your child is phasing out of this stage and into the next (8 to 14 months), things can be hidden under a pillow, in your hand, or under a blanket. At first when you play this game, the object should always be partly in view.

A final way to ensure the growth of intelligence during this period is to verbalize often and simply about the experiences your baby is having. As you talk about the toys he's playing with, you'll give him the idea that objects have labels, things have names. Name the toy and describe its shape, color, characteristics, and perhaps the sound it makes. Talk about what your child is doing *to* or doing *with* the object. Such conversation, even

though only one-way, helps the baby realize words are linked with things. And your monologue reinforces his interest in a toy or a pattern of play, perhaps stimulating further experimentation with it.

BEHAVIORS and ABILITIES

Every time a baby exhibits a new motor skill, she sheds a limitation. The history of her physical development is a story of increasing freedom. First she gains head control, mastery over her hands, and the ability to roll over. Then she learns to sit up and crawl. These motor skills offer her new opportunities to educate herself. They help her explore from different perspectives the world around her and its treasure trove of objects.

This stage is the last period when your baby will stay fairly close to the spot where you park her. She may inch backward a bit or get up on hands and knees as if about to take off, but she may not leave the starting block until the end of this stage. If you have a stationary baby, enjoy your peace of mind. On the other hand if you have a very physically active baby, who starts moving about rather nimbly during this stage, be vigilant.

Your child is now able to see quite well across a room and around the backyard or park. She is noticing much that is colorful and interesting in her environs, but she probably can't get to these things on her own yet. You must bring the objects to her so she can benefit from hands-on exploration.

If you place your 6-month-old on a blanket or mat or outside in an expanding corral, leave a few playthings on her special turf for inspection. Our Versatile Triangle, Roly-Polys, and Kaleidescope are ideal for mat play.

During these few months your offspring phases out of a mainly horizontal position and discovers the joys of life in a vertical situation. The ability to sit up gives her refreshing new views of her surroundings. It also offers her new ways to handle playthings and to learn while doing so. She may sit supported in a high chair, at an eating table or play table, or in a walker before she can sit on her own, unsupported by a chair back. Playthings don't have to be placed in the immediate vicinity of your baby's hands now. She can lean forward from a sitting position and grasp things that are a little out of reach. The tray attached to high chairs is a good surface on which to place new objects for examination.

Try a tea infuser or melon baller. Your baby will probably become totally absorbed with such utensils. See our Serendipity List for suggestions of household items.

Your baby will begin to maneuver toward things quite nearby on the floor or in the playpen in the back of a station wagon by rolling over or creeping forward or backward. Sometimes she locomotes unintentionally or moves backward when she'd really like to go forward for a toy. You may have to help out by shoving the toy a little nearer. But occasionally you may place a toy a little out of reach so that her getting her hands on it becomes a mini-challenge.

Babies become mobile in a variety of ways. Some propel themselves forward by their arms, dragging their tummies along the ground. Some get up on all four's and just rock back and forth before learning to crawl. Some move backward quite ably before they move forward. Some never crawl at all but scoot along on their behind. Style doesn't matter, but getting there does. Don't leave your baby too long in a high chair, walker, or playpen. Place her in the middle of a room where some toys are within reach and where some are out of reach. Curiosity about those farther-away objects will gradually be a great motivator for mobility.

Your budding gymnast is using her leg muscles more and more. Leg thrusts are powerful, and toys to kick or push against will be a source of great pleasure. The kick toys described in the last chapter may still be of interest during this stage.

Walkers can be exciting vehicles for leg-thrusters, but they require extra vigilance on the part of parents. Don't put your child in one unless you have the time to observe closely while she "covers the waterfront." The educational payoff is her opportunity to touch and study at close range many things like shiny doorknobs and knobby table legs that she would otherwise only see from afar. It may relieve the possible frustration a chubby baby feels who cannot yet crawl to all the lovely things she sees and wants to touch.

Physically active babies may pull themselves up to a standing position at the end of this phase. They hold onto their crib rail and soon sidestep along the mattress.

INTERESTS

During the previous stage—3½ to 5½ months—as your baby developed the art of reaching and grasping, he watched his hands a lot as they touched objects. During this phase—5½ to 8 months—a baby tends to watch the effects which his hands have upon the objects. In other words, earlier your baby watched the motor act itself; now he watches the effect of his motor act.

Your baby drops objects off his high chair tray and throws them out of the playpen. When he does this repeatedly, a parent or caregiver who has to retrieve the flying objects finds the behavior irritating. However, think of it this way: your baby is experimenting with cause-and-effect relationships. He's interested in the effect of releasing the object he's been holding in his hands. He may watch it drop or, if he can't see it, he listens to the click or thud of its collision with the floor. He may watch the object roll or wobble away from the playpen. He seems to be studying the consequences of his hand movements. Tennis Anyone? and Sponge and Feather Flings are toys styled to suit this behavior.

The infant experimenter also listens to the effects of his actions. He's aware of sound effects that he creates by banging objects against different surfaces. He may blink and wince at some of the loud sounds he makes, but he keeps on banging anyway.

"What happens when . . . ?" appears to be a question a baby of this age is asking himself. What happens when I hit the measuring cup with a spoon, or when I knock over the tower of blocks Dad built?

Your baby may appreciate in a vague way that the cause-and-effect process sometimes involves a linked series of steps. He may muse to himself (nonverbally, of course): "First, I drop a spool. Then it bangs the floor. Then it rolls. Then it hits a cabinet and stops. Then it stays still." He is learning, learning, learning about the physical world he's in.

His preoccupation with cause-and-effect relationships makes him intrigued with simple mechanisms like light switches and vacuum cleaner on-off buttons. You can search your house for devices that will delight him: for example, the tub stopper, the sink faucet, a light dimmer switch, a door latch. Push, pull, press, lift . . . something happens. At first you can work the gadget for him. Later, if he can manage to work it himself, let him have the thrill of being the cause of a satisfying effect.

Small objects continue to be of great interest to a baby. He appears to be investigating their physical properties. He notices their color, texture, shape, and hardness or softness. He observes how they move or change shape when squeezed or whether they make noises when shaken.

Your little one will automatically reach for any small object you hold up 3 to 8 inches from his hands. If you hold it a bit farther away, he will even lean forward to grasp it, usually with his right hand. Now is the time to start building a collection of these graspable, droppable, throwable objects. Keep them in one or more containers such as our decorated Pail Pal or a large round cookie tin. Instructions for these are given in Chapter Five.

These small treasures can be objects you make according to patterns in this book, toys you buy, household utensils you borrow from your own drawers, hardware or stationery store gadgets, throwaway items from retail or industrial firms, thingamajigs you happen on by chance, and bits and pieces you ferret out of Grandma's wastebasket. (See our Serendipity List.) All objects should pass a rigorous safety test: no rough surfaces or sharp edges, no parts easily broken off, nothing swallowable, all parts colorfast and nontoxic. This valuable collection, begun now, will continue to be a source of fascination until your connoisseur reaches at least 15 months of age.

A few more specific interests complete the repertoire of curiosities belonging to a baby 5½ to 8 months old. It's still worthwhile keeping a mirror over your baby's changing table, even though his interest in mirrors is probably waning now.

Balls of various sizes begin to be quite entertaining during this stage. There are 2 reasons for their success: a baby can make a ball travel far even though he only manages to give it a little push or a clumsy throw, and a ball that has rolled away gives a baby a perfect excuse to show off his budding skill of creeping or crawling to retrieve it.

Whereas your child's focus centered on his hands in the last phase, a focus on his feet develops during this stage. He is interested in the effects he can create with his foot movements. Try placing a beach ball in the vicinity of his feet and note the exhilaration he feels kicking it.

SAFETY NOTE

Use a ruler to measure the diameter of objects you give your baby. If they are 1¼" or over in diameter and 2¼" in depth, they cannot be swallowed. Check larger objects to be sure no small parts of dangerous size could break off.

28. Versatile Triangle

Reason for Toy

A sitting baby or one still enjoying life in a horizontal position can find many ways to play with this lightweight, interestingly shaped object. He can shove it around the floor, pick it up, place it on one side, or stand it on end. He can thrust a fist through the center or whack it against an armchair. Versatility extends the interest value of a toy.

Materials

corrugated cardboard from cartons
aluminum foil
picture cut from magazine or drawn with felt-tip pen
patterned Con-Tact paper
transparent Con-Tact paper
cloth tape, 1½" wide
1 dozen large paper clips
Elmer's Glue-All

Instructions

1. Cut strip of cardboard 16" x 7¾". Cut another 15¾" x 7¾".
2. Divide cardboard in thirds and score lightly with mat knife or single-edged razor blade.

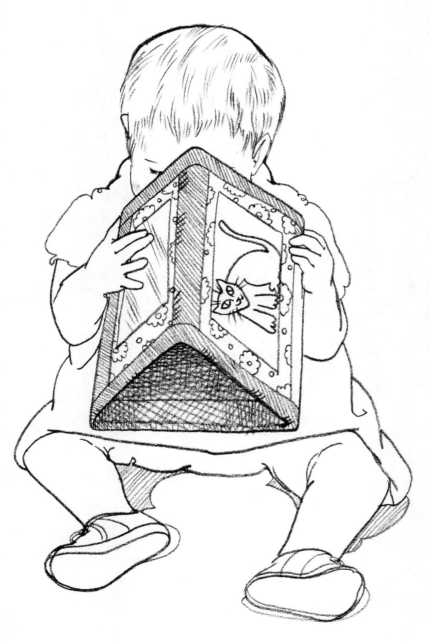

3. Fold cardboard strips into triangles, bending along scores. Spread outside of smaller one liberally with glue. Laminate strips together; outside triangle will hold inside one closed. Use several large paper clips to hold triangles together while drying overnight. The double layer provides strength and durability.
4. On one side center a rectangle of aluminum foil held on by a larger piece of transparent Con-Tact.
5. On another side center a clear bright picture drawn with felt-tip pen or cut out of a magazine. Adhere it with more transparent Con-Tact paper.
6. Cut 3 rectangles of patterned Con-Tact paper to cover sides of triangle. Cut windows in 2 of rectangles to let the picture and foil show through. Cover all sides. Bind all edges with cloth tape.

How to Use

Lay this triangle on mattress or floor mat for playtime. For a toddler, hide a toy inside or drop a toy through center when holding triangle on a slant. He can watch toy disappear and then reappear out the other end.

5½ to 8 Months: Experimenting with Cause and Effect

29. Tube Twins

Reason for Toy

Here are fun objects that a sitting baby can lean forward and reach for or that a creeping baby can inch along the floor toward. She can easily learn about cause and effect with them because when she pushes, they roll. They can begin her collection of small, graspable, throwable objects.

Materials

2 empty toilet-paper rolls
2 empty paper-towel rolls
2 swatches from differently patterned fabrics
Elmer's Glue-All

Instructions

1. Cut 2 rectangles from one fabric, both about 4½" x 5". Cover toilet-paper rolls with rectangles, gluing fabric to cardboard.

2. Cut 2 rectangles from the other fabric, both about 5½" x 11". Glue these to paper-towel rolls.

How to Use

Hand your baby a tube, holding it a little out of reach so she has to lean forward to grasp it. Then hand her another and watch what she does with the first. Does she put it in her lap? Does she drop it or transfer it to the other hand? Hand her a third tube. Does she let go of one, both, or manage to hold all 3? Try this sequence from time to time and again when she is older. It's fun to see how babies cope with a series of objects handed them.

 Lay all 4 rolls in the playpen to engage your tot while you mop the floor, answer the phone, or bury yourself in the newspaper.

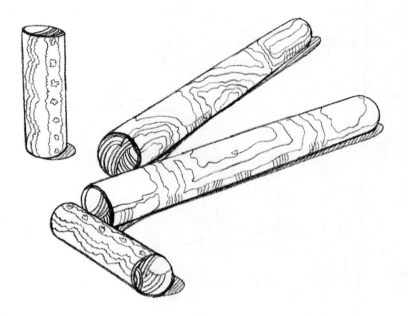

30. Spool Circle

Reason for Toy

This toy can be banged on the floor or knocked against hard things to produce satisfying claps. Babies often enjoy such loud noises. The spools can be gummed by teething babies.

Materials

several empty wooden or plastic spools of thread, not styrofoam
large wooden beads (optional)
ribbon or heavyweight string, about 12″ long

Instructions

1. String spools and a couple of wooden beads, if you like, on a ribbon or string.
2. Tie the ends together to form a circle.

How to Use

Place on floor mat or in bath. Or you could reserve this toy together with a few other playthings to bring out only when you visit friends or relatives. Its novelty then should guarantee interest. A baby engrossed in his toys is a welcome guest, and you can enjoy the luxury of uninterrupted conversation.

Safety Note

This toy is not meant to fit over the head. For safety's sake keep the circle small enough to use just for holding. When your baby gums the spools, be sure he is not biting into the edges. Some plastic spools could crack, and wooden spools might splinter.

31. Kaleidoscope

Reason for Toy

Shaking, as well as dropping and throwing, teaches a baby that she can be the cause of an effect. Shaking this audiovisual toy produces both rattling sounds and changing patterns. An advantage of this box is the chance it offers to play with very small objects which, if not encased, would be withheld because they are easily swallowed.

Materials

strong transparent plastic box (about 3″ x 4½″), with 6 storage
    compartments (available at hardware or variety store)
brass button
5 little balls of crinkled-up foil
feather
some glittering sequins or bread or cake crumbs
unpopped corn
colored wooden bead
cloth tape

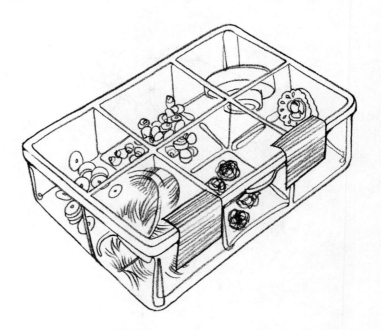

Instructions

1. Into each compartment put an object or group of things such as those listed above.
2. Tape box firmly closed.

How to Use

Try keeping this box handy in the car glove compartment to change the mood of a testy baby during traffic jams.

Variation

Babies of this age like to stare at tiny particles such as the sequins in this box. Since they put everything in the mouth, you must be careful of the tiny things they see and want to taste—for instance, bugs! As a safe alternative, place a pile of cake crumbs or a melange of brown and white bread crumbs on the high chair tray for your baby to scrutinize.

Safety Note

Look for any signs of the box cracking as a result of your baby's banging it against hard surfaces. Check often to be sure tape is holding. You do not want the small objects inside to spill out where she could pick them up and put them in her mouth.

32. Roly-Polys

Reason for Toy

With only a little shove, babies can launch these cylinders into a forward roll. The rock-filled container flops forward and backward in a provocatively peculiar manner. Babies always prefer a moving toy to a stationary one. The cylinders won't roll far though, and the desire to handle them again may give even the chubbiest baby incentive to inch forward.

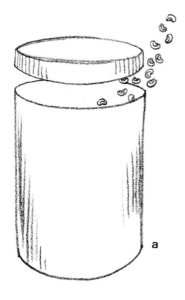

a

b

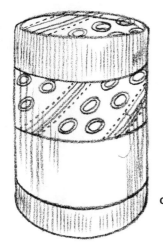

c

Materials

1 full cylindrical salt box
3 empty cylindrical salt boxes
handful of lentils or peanuts
several nails
a large rock
patterned Con-Tact paper
cloth tape

Instructions

1. With sharp knife, cut off the tops of the empty boxes about ½″ from the end.
2. Put lentils or peanuts in one, nails in another, and a rock in the third (a). (The heavy box, full of salt, rolls differently.)
3. Place the tops back in position on boxes. Cut 3 circles of Con-Tact paper big enough to cover the ends of each box and the seams where the cut-off tops meet the bottoms. After slitting the Con-Tact edge every ½″ (so that it fits around the box better), adhere it over top and across seam in each box. Cover the bottoms of the boxes too, if you wish (b).
4. Place strip of tape around seam to make sure top won't come off. For appearance, add more strips of Con-Tact or tape around the body of the boxes (c).

How to Use

Stack the lightweight cylinders. Your impish offspring will delight in knocking down your tower.

33. Egg-Rolling Contest

Reason for Toy

These eggs can be shaken, clicked together, thrown (on a rug), or pushed around with equally satisfying results. The strings help a relatively stationary baby to retrieve an egg which has rolled away.

Materials

Use the toys which you made for Easter Egg Hunt in Chapter Two, but trim the strings short. If you did not make that toy, obtain the materials listed there and follow instructions (but don't tie the eggs to the dowel).

How to Use

Lay eggs on floor mat or rug for your baby to play with when he is lying on his back, stomach, or side, or is sitting up.

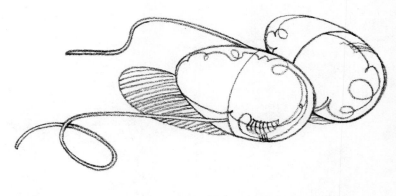

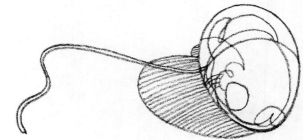

34. Tennis Anyone?

Reason for Toy

Your Galilean infant now studies the effect of her motor act on an object. She drops or throws something in order to watch the resulting fall or roll. Also, a desire to practice her newfound ability to release a grasped toy makes her drop or throw it again and again.

Materials

old tennis ball
heavyweight string, about 24″ long
sleigh bell (optional)

Instructions

1. Using a mat knife, make a small slit (about ¾″ wide) in tennis ball.
2. Tie several knots close together at the end of string.
3. Using a dull table knife, poke the knotted end of the string through the slit into the tennis ball. This will be hard to do, but once in, it will not pull back out.
4. You may push a sleigh bell into slit too.

How to Use

So that you will not be forever retrieving thrown objects, tie the end of the string to the tray of the high chair and hand your baby the ball. Your tennis ace will have a built-in ball boy (see illustration for Sponge and Feather Flings).

Variation

You may also dangle this ball from a kitchen drawer handle. Pull out the drawer a few inches, then, when your baby sits on the floor, she can bat it back and forth like a tether ball. This will keep her busy while you're on the telephone.

Safety Note

Supervise the play so that your baby does not get tangled in string; you can keep it rather short for safety.

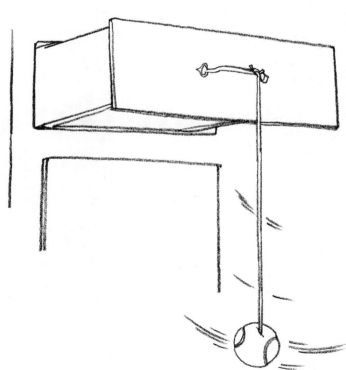

5½ to 8 Months: Experimenting with Cause and Effect

35. Sponge and Feather Flings

Reason for Toy

Monitoring the movements of a thrown object intrigues your junior physicist. Feathers waft, sponges plop, he notes, if given a chance to experiment with these toys.

Sponge Fling

Materials

3 small ovals of colored sponges, about 2″ in diameter
lightweight string

Instructions

1. Wash sponges (as commercial ones are impregnated with a bad-tasting substance).
2. Poke string through sponges with an ice pick or thread a very large-eyed needle with string and pull it through.
3. Tie sponges together in a cluster at end of string.
4. Cut string about 24″ long.

Feather Fling

Materials

several feathers
lightweight string
Elmer's Glue-All

Instructions

1. Glue feathers together at quill ends.
2. While glue is wet, tie a string tightly around quill ends and apply more glue. Let dry.
3. Cut string about 24" long.

How to Use

Tie string ends to side bars of high chair and lay toys on tray. After examining objects, your baby will drop, shove, or throw them off. Help with retrievals at first, and by 8 months your baby will reel in the fallen toys himself.

Variations

You can also give balled-up paper and the small cardboard boxes that cosmetics come in for different throwing experiences.

36. Rock 'n' Roll Drums

Reason for Toy

Banging, like throwing and shaking, is one of the principal manual operations of the 6+-month-old baby. This set of drums offers different surfaces to hit—one cardboard, one metal—which produce hollow thuds and tinny clashes. Banging teaches about the properties of objects.

Materials

1 large tin can with one end removed
1 or 2 spoons (wooden or plastic)
1 large cylindrical oatmeal box with one end removed
Con-Tact paper, brightly colored or patterned
cloth tape

Instructions

1. Cut oatmeal box down to be about 7″ high.
2. Cover outside of box with Con-Tact paper and extend paper over rim 1 or 2 inches down into inside.
3. Cover open end of tin can with Con-Tact paper, slitting edges every ½″ so it can fit around can smoothly.
4. Tape around Con-Tact on outside of can to hold it firmly in place.

How to Use

Offer only 1 drum at first. After your musician gets used to it, introduce the second. The tin-can drum and spoon fit inside oatmeal drum for storage. Real interest in using these objects as drums develops more fully in the next age bracket. Right now her banging is random and is combined with other ways of exploring the toys.

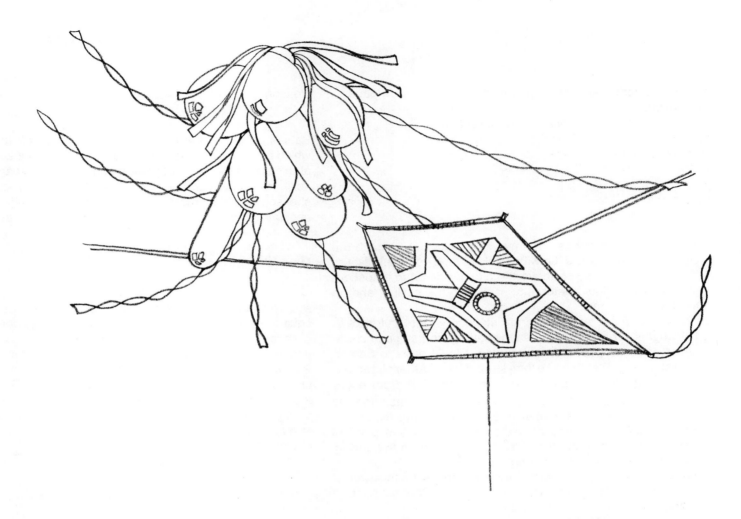

37. Happy Un-Birthday!

Reason for Toy

Now that your baby can see across a room and is no longer oriented only to things 3 or 4 feet away, surprise him with some festive scenery to gaze at. While he's outside or sleeping, decorate the ceiling and wall high above his bed.

Materials

balloons
10 crepe-paper streamers or streamers cut from tissue paper
kite (optional)
suction-cup hook and liquid detergent (optional)
masking tape
lightweight string

Instructions

1. Blow up some balloons. Tie them in a cluster and attach the cluster to a light fixture. Or with masking tape you could fasten them to the ceiling just above the crib. Or dampen a suction-cup hook with liquid detergent, stick it to the ceiling, and tie the balloons to that.
2. Use crepe-paper streamers from stationery store cut in 6' to 10' lengths. Or make streamers by cutting long strips of crepe paper or tissue paper about 3" wide. (You'll have to Scotch tape strips together to make long streamers.) Gather streamers together at one end and tie with string about 2' from edge.
3. Tape this string to the ceiling where you have fastened the balloons so that the streamer ends hang down to flutter.
4. Fan out the other ends of the streamers, twisting pairs of them a little and letting them sag down a bit from the ceiling. Tape far ends to wall or ceiling.
5. You can also buy a colorful kite and tape it to the wall or ceiling in addition to or as a substitute for the balloons. It will further enliven the decoration.

38. Peek-a-Boo

Reason for Toy

Babies delight at the reappearance of a familiar face or object which has disappeared. This accounts for the unqualified success at this age of the game of peek-a-boo. Toward 1 year, your baby's ability to remember a missing object develops. It could be said she solves an elementary problem when she lifts the curtain obscuring the face in order to have another look at it.

Materials

square piece of cardboard, about 11" on each side
square piece of fabric, about 9½" on each side, cut with pinking shears
construction paper, same size as cardboard
2 coaster-size paper doilies (optional)
cloth tape
2 pieces of yarn or string, about 18" long
transparent Con-Tact paper
strong yarn
felt-tip pen

Instructions

1. Draw a face or picture of something your child likes on a piece of colored construction paper. (You may glue on doilies for a lace collar.)
2. Lay this piece of paper on the cardboard and cover the whole thing with Con-Tact paper, folding Con-Tact around sides of cardboard onto the back.
3. Tape the cloth along top edge of cardboard so it covers the picture.
4. With a paper punch make holes near the top 2 corners.
5. Thread yarn through these holes.

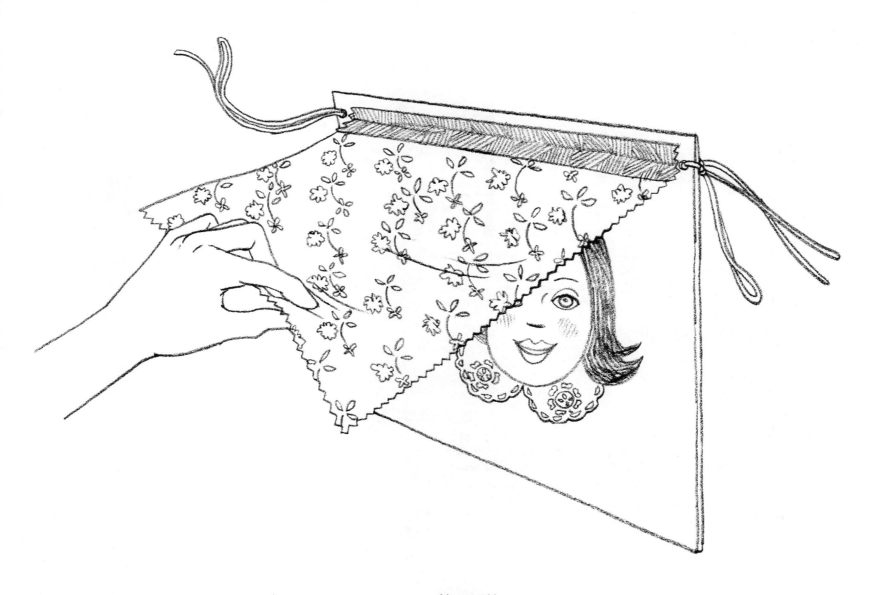

How to Use

Tie game to crib or playpen rail for independent investigation. When together with baby, hold cardboard and flip curtain up and down with appropriate exclamations such as "All gone!" and "Peek-a-boo!"

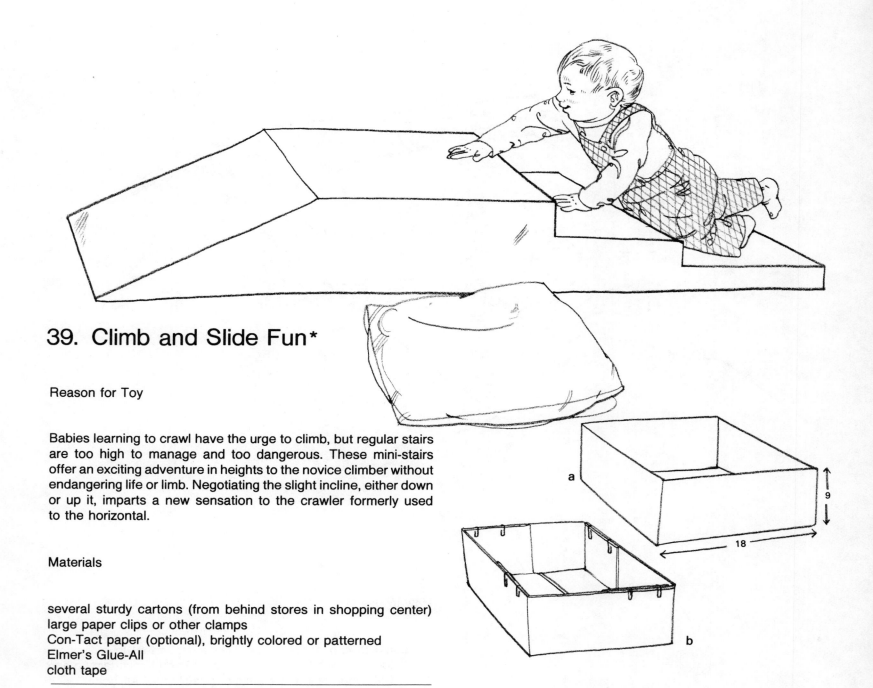

39. Climb and Slide Fun*

Reason for Toy

Babies learning to crawl have the urge to climb, but regular stairs are too high to manage and too dangerous. These mini-stairs offer an exciting adventure in heights to the novice climber without endangering life or limb. Negotiating the slight incline, either down or up it, imparts a new sensation to the crawler formerly used to the horizontal.

Materials

several sturdy cartons (from behind stores in shopping center)
large paper clips or other clamps
Con-Tact paper (optional), brightly colored or patterned
Elmer's Glue-All
cloth tape

a

9

18

b

* Design concept originated by Burton L. White

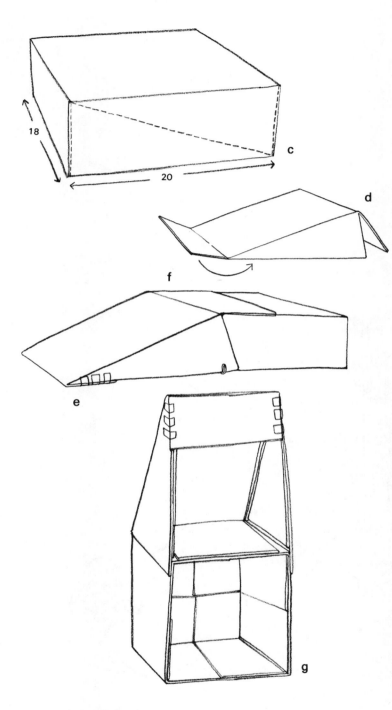

Instructions

The object is to have three 3″-high stairs. The other dimensions can vary according to the sizes of the cartons you're able to collect.

1. Start with a large carton and trim the top edges to make the sides 9″ deep. The model was 18″ square (a).
2. Reinforce this, and all other boxes used in this climber, by gluing to all inside surfaces another layer of cardboard (cut from other cartons). For example, inside this first box glue 4 pieces of corrugated cardboard, each 9″ by 18″. Fold each piece in half and glue in a different corner inside the box, laying half on the bottom and half running up the side. Weigh down with heavy books and clamp edges with paper clips until glue dries. Leave several hours or overnight (b).
3. Cut another carton on the diagonal as shown in figure (c), preserving ends, and slit all corners (d). The model was 20″ long, 18″ wide. Close one flap under and tape in place (e). The other flap helps connect this carton with first carton. Using a generous layer of glue, adhere ramp to first carton, which becomes the top step or center platform (f). Weigh down glued section with books and clamp with paper clips until glue dries.
4. Turn over and reinforce all inside of ramp with another layer of cardboard pieces (g). Let dry.
5. Generously glue a 6″-deep box to the side of your original carton opposite the ramp. This makes the middle step.
6. Glue a 3″-deep box to the side of the 6″-deep one to finish the stairs. Let dry well.
7. Cover the entire climber with Con-Tact paper if you want to give it more visual appeal.

How to Use

Place pillows along both sides of structure until your baby can maneuver steps smoothly. Place baby in front of steps, and let him mount them. He'll slide down the ramp on his tummy or on all four's. Help him not to slide too fast down the ramp and bump his nose.

Another time, place him at the foot of the ramp and let him try to mount it. If he slips back, support him. You may place a toy on the center platform as a reward.

Chapter Five

8 to 14 Months:
Exploring Places
and Examining Things

EDUCATION

To do right by your child educationally during this period is quite
a challenge. Parents find it hard to cope with a baby who's "into
everything," messing up every square foot of the house and often
endangering herself. Theoretically, a parent wants to encourage
a child to investigate because that's the way a child learns. But
practically, it's a strain to permit the thorough investigation typical
of the baby who's just learned to crawl.

Babies are extraordinarily curious. How to foster that curiosity
without letting the child hurt herself or the house is a fine art.
Parents worry about the safety of their child and the preservation
of the decor, but such worry can cause a mother or father to
so over-restrict or over-protect an offspring that the baby's curiosity becomes dulled. A baby constantly curtailed by "no-no's" begins to feel that her parents' disapproval refers not just to specific
things or areas but to the act of examination itself. Nothing could

be more harmful to intellectual development.

Curiosity is the single most important quality that will help your child be an eager learner later in school. Therefore it is essential to safeguard curiosity during these tender months when it is first blossoming. You can do this by letting your baby roam in as many areas of your home as possible. You can talk in a friendly and enthusiastic way about her meanderings around the house and her discoveries en route. You can encourage your caregiver, if you have one, to do so also. And you can supply the types of toys and household objects that match your baby's current interests and abilities.

Freedom from the playpen and access to 1 or more rooms is possible if you "baby-proof" these rooms. Careful baby-proofing or accident-proofing will give you peace of mind and relieve you of the burden of constantly surveying and restricting dangerous exploits. And your child won't hear "no" or feel a little slap every time she turns around and touches something.

Before your baby starts crawling, try analyzing your house with the objectivity of a safety inspector, and then make changes. You might drop to your hands and knees to get a truer perspective of the territory your crawler will roam. Anything small and swallowable under your couch or dresser? Can knobs on your TV or stereo be pulled off?

Systematically go around stripping your home of delicate ornaments; taping sharp corners of low coffee tables; emptying low (and later high) cabinets of poisonous products, such as floor and sink cleansing agents; capping electric outlets; and so on. And the items under that label "and so on" may be the most important, although they may differ from house to house!

Decide on where you store sharply pointed things like pencils, pens, and tools. Be aware of what you drop into an open wastebasket or kitchen garbage bag. If you don't consider plants or books on a low shelf fair game for a baby's direct aim, you should remove them—just for a year or so. Gates or blockades of some sort should keep staircases and parents' project areas out of bounds.

While your baby is still stationary, you may not realize how much mischief she can get into once off and running. So during the first week of real mobility, watch her like a hawk and see what redesigning still needs to be done to accommodate your small floor-hugger.

The instinct to examine is so strong at this age and the memory for an instruction such as "don't touch" so short that

baby-proofing seems to be the only fair solution. Pride in interior decoration and some conveniences of adult life-style must be set aside for the time being.

There will always be a few untouchables that, for some reason, cannot be eliminated. When your daughter approaches these, you may use the occasion to teach her the meaning of the word *no*. Part of her education is to realize that a home has rules, life contains do's and don't's, and parents are authority figures who, in a friendly but firm way, set limits.

You'll enjoy this superactive stage more if you realize that a well-developing crawler naturally creates clutter. If her movements through the house did not result in a trail of debris, there would be something wrong. So talk yourself and your spouse into tolerating some clutter for the sake of your offspring's cognitive development! Occasionally gather the toys and deposit them in accessible containers. Then let your child begin again the process of picking up and casting aside attractive objects.

The best thing that can happen to any baby is her parents' delight in her exploring of places and examining of things. If you provide an affectionate background for her rovings and show excitement over her discoveries, she will be hooked on learning for life.

MORE ON EDUCATION

When you introduce a toy or a group of toys to your baby or when you play a game like peek-a-boo, there is a good rule to follow to make the experience more educational. First, let the baby become familiar with the toy or set of toys. Or let him get used to the basic way of playing the game. Then, instead of introducing a totally different toy or starting a whole new game to amuse him, just make a small change in the familiar toy or game. This approach could be called creating a "variation on a theme."*

Composers have long done this with music. They make up a tune, called a theme, and then invent variations on the theme

---

* This concept stems from research done by Jerome Kagan, Ph.D., at the Center for Cognitive Studies in Cambridge, Ma.

which are repetitions of the tune with modifications in rhythm, harmony, melody, or key. As your baby's playmate, you or the caregiver are like a composer creating a theme. You play it until your "listener," the baby, is familiar with it and just beginning to get bored with it. Then you play variations on the theme.

For example, a child enjoys dropping small objects into an open coffee can. After he has observed this phenomenon of gravity over and over again, his interest is rekindled if you change the toy slightly. Put a lid on it and cut a hole in the top. Now he has to drop the objects through the opening. It's a "whole new ball game."

The same rule works for a game like peek-a-boo. Play it the normal way so that your hands open revealing your face. After you've played it this way for a week, try a variation. Hold a diaper in front of your face, then let it drop. Your baby's interest in the game will be renewed.

A slight change in an already familiar game is more interesting to your baby than an entirely new game. One reason this is true is that your baby has an inborn inclination to figure out the unfamiliar in his experience. He likes a slight discrepancy or deviation from the normal pattern and feels himself learning from it. Educating your baby at this age involves thinking up changes in the play situation that would cause patterns of play to vary.

You can prolong interest in the toys in this book by occasionally altering their appearance in some way or changing a component part. For instance, a set of small objects usually kept in a pail can be transferred to a basket for a new look. In many cases we suggest variations. Often the altering of a familiar toy is more intriguing than a brand-new toy.

You will notice, as your baby grows, that he invents his own variations on a theme by playing with a toy in new ways. You set the example for such creativity when you apply this rule from time to time as you guide your baby's play experiences.

BEHAVIORS

Your baby is now going to divide her busy day into 3 activities. One is watching you and deciphering your facial expressions, body language, and words. A second activity, and one she spends much more time on, is exploring her house on her hands and knees and examining all the objects in it—utilitarian and decorative household objects as well as toys. A third activity is mastering her own motor skills.

During the first activity she's learning about what kind of person you are: generally friendly, loving, and approving but also firm. She's learning all the can's and cannot's, the should's and shouldn't's—the rulebook according to Mom or Dad. Your child comes often to you during this stage for comfort in distress, for assistance with a little problem, or for an enthusiastic response when she is pleased about something. The way you respond to these overtures sets the tone for this first important social relationship with another human being. A very strong, close bond gets established with the primary caregiver whether the person is father, mother, or daily baby-sitter.

The second activity of exploring the world around her is the result of a baby's sudden mobility. New crawlers are like Lewis and Clark on expedition, mapping the geography of their home. Part of the exploration process is the examining of all the details of your furnishings, the ordinary household objects within reach, and the toys you may keep in each room. Educational researchers have observed that 1-year-olds spend almost 15 percent of their time examining the characteristics of objects. The proportion of time spent on this preoccupation is large compared to that spent on any other single pastime.

The third activity in your older baby's busy day is the mastering of motor skills. Your daughter has a drive to perfect whatever is the currently developing muscular skill. During this dynamic phase of growth, you will be in awe of the changes. Before she's 14 months old she will crawl, climb, pull herself to a standing position, cruise (walk sideways holding on to something), walk unaided, and possibly run. She is also practicing increasingly complicated digital skills.

Your child is never satisfied with her first clumsy efforts at these new gross-motor skills. She demands perfection of herself. Never conscious of the laboriousness of repeating these efforts over and over again, she just glories in the increasing freedom she is gaining.

It's going to seem to you as if your baby is always on the move, but researchers have noticed that babies of this age also spend a lot of time simply staring. They stare in order to gain information. Sometimes they are obviously listening as well as watching, both actions for the purpose of gaining information about the scene before them. They will stare at their mother or father working around the house. They'll look out the window or watch other children at play. They will study a toy just before or just after banging it on a table or throwing it.

At 1 year of age their good vision enables them to see fine detail accurately. Therefore they like not only the natural-wood or solid-colored toy, but also the plaything that has detailed graphic decoration on it. They even stare at tiny specks such as bits of sawdust. The ability to sit up enhances their tendency to stare because the upright posture facilitates the ability to observe.

ABILITIES

Parents marvel at their child's first signs of understanding words. At 7 or 8 months a baby begins to realize that words have meanings. At 9 or 10 months he may understand up to 10 specific words. When a baby first complies with simple requests like "wave bye-bye" or "clap hands," his parents find it hard to contain their joy and rapture. Nor should they!

It is very important now to start talking simply about the object your child is playing with. First, name it: "That's a cup." Then describe its characteristics: "It's smooth and orange." Describe what your baby is doing with it: "You're putting that ball in the cup." Suggest something else to do with the object and, in the spirit of fun, see if he complies with the request: "Put the cup on the table."

Around 12 to 14 months, a baby speaks his first words. But how many words he *says* at this age is not nearly as significant as how many words he *understands*. Understanding words is the key to good language development. To encourage understanding, just talk simply and sociably about the thing or act or event that your baby is paying attention to at any given moment.

Locomotion is the trademark of the 8- to 14-month-old. He changes dramatically at the beginning of this phase from a sedentary creature lying on a mat just looking at everything to a mobile creature propelling himself off the mat, across the room, and into other rooms. After your baby has learned to crawl, he soon learns to climb, first 6-inch units (stairs), then 12-inch units (stools), soon chairs and chairbacks! The parent or caregiver turns into a constant bodyguard. Staircases seem to draw a baby like a magnet. Clambering up an ottoman is like scaling Mt. Everest, but getting that body entirely off the ground and onto a piece of furniture is a heady experience. Your baby will thrive on such altitude.

All too quickly he gives up locomoting on hands and knees. He begins to pull himself to a standing position by means of the crib or playpen rail or by a piece of furniture. Once having achieved the standing position, he begins to sidestep or walk holding on to the rail or the chair, couch, or table edge. This supported sidestepping is called "cruising" by baby observers. Just before or soon after the first birthday, your "special" baby will perform that un-special but always spellbinding act—walking forward totally on his own.

As if such a sequence of physical events wasn't enough change within a 6-month period to exhaust the flexibility of any parent, there are 2 final gross-motor skills often achieved by 14 months of age: the ability to run, and the capacity to straddle and maneuver small 4-wheeled vehicles designed for the toddler.

At the same time as your baby is exhibiting such dramatic progress in the gross-motor skills, he is also developing his fine-motor skills. His fingers become more dextrous daily. At first, he examines objects with his thumb and all fingers. Then you notice he practices a pincer grip on things; that is, he grasps with the thumb and forefinger. Later he uses just 1 finger to poke, touch, press, or rub an object.

This regular handling of small objects of various sizes and shapes is preparing him for more complicated future activities with his hands, such as building a tower of blocks, setting up a town or fort inhabited by small plastic figures, drawing or painting, and finally writing. Without those toddler hours spent in practicing digital skills on odd little 3-dimensional objects, he couldn't learn to write with ease in the early grades.

A lot of your child's fine-motor skills are aimed at discovering the physical attributes of objects. He does this by holding and gumming them, turning them over to see them from a different angle, or perhaps striking them against a surface. During this period he becomes a junior physicist, manually discovering whether things are soft and floppy or hard and flat or perhaps round and smooth. He begins to understand which things will stack, which will roll, which will stand up. These discoveries are important to the construction activities undertaken during the nursery school years.

Besides using his senses of touch and taste to learn the properties of objects, he likes to exercise skills that show his mastery over the objects. He puts things in and draws them out of containers. He pours. He takes apart toys and, once in a while, puts them together. He fits one object onto another. He slides one gadget into another. He pushes a lever. He swings back and forth an object on hinges. He throws and rolls, and then retrieves. It's fun to be master of the physical world; play is proof of that to a toddler.

INTERESTS

During this period of exploration of the interior landscape of your home a child spends little time with commercial toys. The furnishings of a house are far more fascinating: the baseboard heating fenders, the low picture-window sills, the fringe on the rug, the dust puffs under the couch, the hemline of the drapes, and the fireplace tools. Getting to know each nook and cranny seems an obsession. What your baby was once able to see only from afar, he can now suddenly move close to for hands-on examination. An intoxicating experience!

You may be wondering exactly what kind of objects your baby will prefer during this period. Usually small things that fit into a toddler-sized hand will be most appreciated. They should be colorful, sometimes patterned, and irregularly shaped. She likes things with interesting indentations or protuberances. She enjoys things that make a noise. Whether they click, crackle, ding, or rattle matters not; any sound will receive an A-1 rating. She also prefers objects with parts that move; for example, those that slide back and forth, wiggle, vibrate, sway or change form. Keep your eyes open for such gadgets in stationery, hardware, and variety stores or gift shops. A toy store isn't your only resource for safe and pleasing playthings. (See also our Serendipity List.)

Hinged objects hold a peculiar fascination for the 8- to 12-month-old. This preference may be noticeable in the way your baby opens and closes a Band-Aid box with a hinged lid. She may flip back and forth the stiff page of a cardboard book. Certainly you will find her swinging the kitchen cabinet door to and fro on many a day. We include in this chapter a pattern for a toy called Hinged Clappers.

Favorite objects are also those found behind that swinging door: plastic containers, pots, pans, and their lids. You can turn over 1 low cabinet to your child for her own cubbyhole and keep some of her favorite safe kitchen utensils and toys there. This chapter opens with an illustration of a cabinet custom-decorated for your small gadget-minded gourmet.

Wealth to a toddler is a collection of 30 to 40 different small objects, not necessarily bought toys. You can have fun building such a collection. We give you quite a few patterns for objects you can make. Others can be found around your own or others' houses—odds and ends that are unwanted or throwaway items. You might snoop around builders' supply stores or factory outlets for the nontoy toy.

A catch-all container is a must. You can amass all the goodies in 1 large container or divide them up into a few smaller containers such as our Pail Pal. Each one could be kept in a different area of the house, wherever your baby is likely to play: kitchen, nursery, living room, patio.

Present a toddler with a container of little treasures and she will take them out 1 at a time, pausing to examine each. She may put each of those she's looked at back, 1 at a time. At first, she may not look at all of them—just several—before being distracted. Another tactic she may employ is to empty all the contents, examine each singly, and then put some back. If she drops them over the rim of the container and hears a clink, she may then peer into the container to study the object once more at rest inside.

One-year-olds are drawn to objects around the house that embody a cause-and-effect mechanism. One of these is the light switch. Flick! It's bright. Flick! It's dark! Flashlights with a very easy-to-work switch are also appealing. So is the dimmer switch for the dining room chandelier.

Toddlers like an old-fashioned drain stopper in the sink. Plug it in the hole; water collects. Yank it out; the water disappears. If they can work these mechanisms themselves, all the better. Then *they* become the cause of an effect. What power they feel, and in the hands of ones so small! A chance now and then to work such mechanisms can be very ego-building.

Other gadgets with the same magic include the flushing handle of the toilet; controls on the TV or radio; electric blanket controls; and doorknobs, latches, and locks. You may not wish your baby to fiddle with such mechanisms whenever she wants to. But when she's in your arms and you are in command, giving her an opportunity to turn on the TV or stereo will produce a very wide smile.

Babies and toddlers are novice hide-and-seek players. The first hide-and-seek game is probably peek-a-boo. A 9-month-old soon learns to jerk away the scarf that hides a face and find Dad's grin behind it. For 1-year-olds, the less subtle the hiding the better. A toddler delights in watching Daddy hide Mommy behind an armchair and then seeking and climactically finding her.

A stuffed animal can be half-hid under a pillow with a bit of it partly in view. The search can be extensive: "No, it's not here. No, it's not there." Finally, when the child cannot postpone the fun of discovery any longer, she pounces on it. You make the game a bit more difficult when you conceal an object completely behind a barrier and yet do it while your child is watching.

The next step is to pretend to hide it under one pillow, then under another, and actually leave it under a third. The more mature toddler persists in the search until she finds it. In a sense, the disappearance of an object poses a problem to be solved. Finding the object is the young thinker's shrewd solution.

Your baby will enjoy playing with the toys described on the following pages, either by herself or with you as her playmate. They are not arranged in a prescribed sequence. They should be of interest at any point in time over the next several months.

40. Cork Chase

Reason for Toy

Water is interesting to a baby, and not only for its cleansing property. With this toy he can learn about buoyancy.

Materials

4 to 5 large and medium-sized corks, approximately 1½″ high and 1¾″ in diameter across top
2 thin corks, ¾″ high and 2″ in diameter across top
lightweight string, about 12″ long

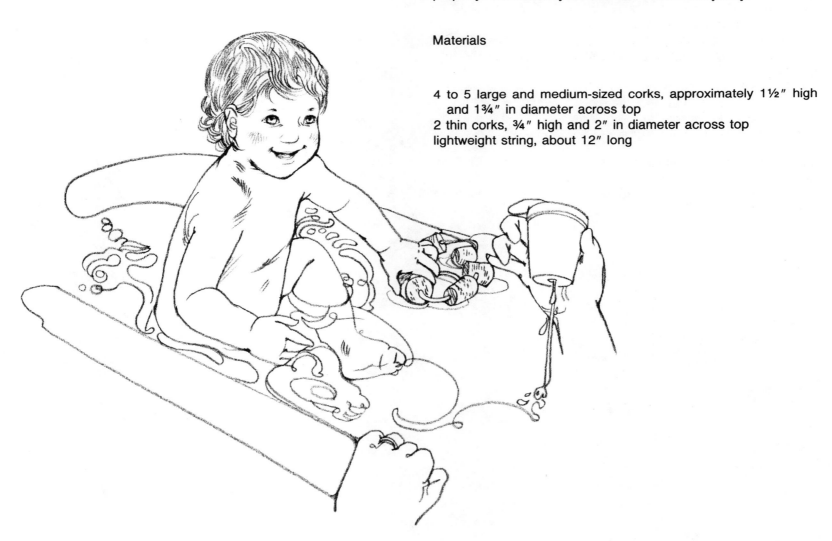

Instructions

1. With an electric or hand drill, make a hole from top to bottom through center of each cork.
2. Thread string through the holes and tie the ends together.

How to Use

A bath can be scheduled just for fun. Toys for water play can be used in wading pool, bathtub, sink, or dishpan on the floor or grass.

Safety Note

Make sure your little bather doesn't chew off bits of cork if this toy comes to the mouth.

When string is only 1' long, toy cannot tangle or be drawn over baby's head.

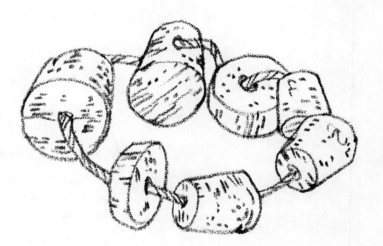

41. Sponge Floater

Reason for Toy

Bathtime is not a routine task for your baby but an aquatic adventure—every time!

Materials

1 brightly colored kitchen sponge
lightweight string, about 12" long

Instructions

1. Wash sponge many times with soap and water and rinse until it is tasteless. (Taste it yourself because it is permeated with a bad-tasting substance that keeps it soft inside its commercial packaging.)
2. When it is tasteless, cut it in 3 pieces with scissors.
3. Poke string through center of each piece with scissors point or ice pick, then tie ends. Circle should not be wide enough to fit over baby's head.

How to Use

Help your baby notice the change in the sponges when they get wet: "First they're dry and hard. Now magic—they're wet and soft!"

Variation

Bring some unbreakable heavy things to the bath area and show your baby how they sink. Later she will enjoy guessing whether things will float or sink.

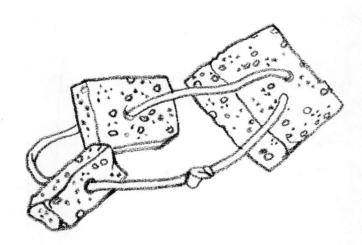

42. Spurt, Squirt, and Trickle Toys

Reason for Toy

Water is a fascinating medium for children because it's so change-
able. Sometimes it drips, sometimes it gushes. It splashes unpre-
dictably. It allows some things to float and others to sink. It's
transparent. Sometimes it's hot, other times cold. Children never
tire of playing with it.

These containers give toddlers a chance to fill and pour,
and then to watch water spurt, squirt, and trickle out of holes.

Materials

2 or 3 empty plastic bottles, for shampoo, dishwashing liquid,
and frozen lemon juice
1 Styrofoam cup
sandpaper
steel wool

Instructions

1. Cut bottles in half, saving the top halves. Sand the edges
   with sandpaper so they are smooth when your baby gums
   them.
2. Scrape the lettering and design off the bottles with steel wool
   and soapy water for safer and handsomer toys.
3. Using ice pick, punch 4 holes in the lid half of your various
   bottles.
4. Punch 1 hole in center of the bottom of the cup.

How to Use

Draw your baby's attention to the bottles with a spout. Show
him how, when pushed closed, it holds water; when pulled open,
it drains. (Older babies pay more attention to the falling water,
whereas younger babies focus more on the container.)

43. Bath-Toy Jug

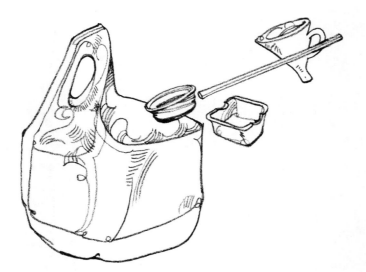

Reason for Toy

This jug can hold all odds and ends for bathtime play. Mom or Dad can fill it with water (heavy!) and empty it, treating baby to a view of a sparkling cascade.

Materials

1-gallon plastic milk bottle
sandpaper

Instructions

1. Cut out wedge of the bottle opposite handle to make scoop shape.
2. Sand edges with sandpaper if sharp.

How to Use

Store in this jug all bath toys made from the preceding patterns. Also add the type of plastic straw used at McDonald's or Burger King.

As your baby gets older, bring to water play area various plastic containers, tops, and lids from your kitchen. Don't forget an egg separator, funnel, colander, or other items with holes or slots that water can flow through.

Safety Note

Supervise bath play vigilantly. A straw is a rather pointed object so be careful of baby's handling of it.

44. Hinged Clappers

Reason for Toy

This toy feeds your baby's curiosity about hinged objects. Grasping the knob and opening and closing these wooden panels are skills your increasingly dextrous baby enjoys performing. Finding the picture inside can be a pleasant surprise over and over again.

Materials

2 pieces of plywood, about 4½" x 6", approximately ⅜" thick
1 piece of fabric, preferably vinyl or stretch, about 4" x 6"
1 round wooden cabinet knob (from hardware store), comes with screw detached
photograph or color picture cut from magazine
acrylic or any other nontoxic paint (optional)
Elmer's Glue-All
sandpaper

Instructions

1. Sand plywood pieces until smooth and splinter-free.
2. The fabric becomes a hinge. Coat it on one side with glue. With the 2 pieces of plywood placed one on top of the other, glue the fabric from the top of one across edges to the bottom of the other (a).
3. Glue wooden knob to plywood across from hinge (b). Discard screw that comes with knob as glue is very strong and easier to use.
4. When knob and hinge have dried, glue a photograph or magazine picture inside for baby to peek at.

How to Use

When you give your baby a toy such as the Clappers, don't have a too precise preconceived notion about how she should play with it. She may handle it in various ways before she gets around to manipulating it the way you have in mind.

Variation

Change the picture surreptitiously. Then observe your baby's reactions upon discovery of the unfamiliar.

45. First Book

Reason for Toy

Babies first see a book as a fascinating hinged object rather than as a book *per se*. Later babies recognize that pictures are symbols of real things, and then they delight at identifying a picture of a familiar scene, object, or person.

Materials

3 white poster boards, 11″ x 14″
brightly colored cloth tape, 1″ wide and 2″ wide
black felt-tip pen
10 clear, rather big pictures from magazines showing things with which your baby is familiar (a doll, cat, dog, child in bathtub, clock, cookies)
transparent Con-Tact paper
Elmer's Glue-All

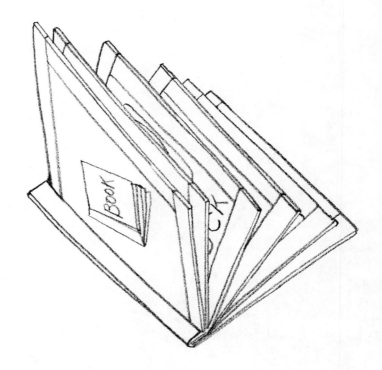

Instructions

1. Cut poster boards in half to make six 5½″ x 7″ pages.
2. In center of each page on both sides paste a picture, leaving 1 page blank for cover. Under each picture print in large, black letters the appropriate word: *cat, clock,* and so forth. On front cover draw a simple picture of a book.
3. Cover both sides of each page with Con-Tact paper to make them drool-proof.
4. Tape around 3 outside edges of each page with 1″-wide tape to make them chew-proof.
5. Along the inside edge of each page, run a piece of 2″-wide tape, half on and half off the edge (a).
6. Lay all 6 pages on top of each other and press tapes together (b).

7. Open the book, and between each pair of facing pages run a length of 1"-wide tape.
8. Run a length of 2"-wide tape, half on front, half on back, to bind outside of book (c).

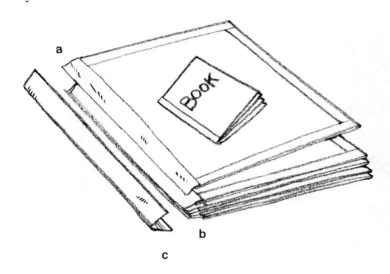

How to Use

Ask your baby, "Where's the cat?" Let her point to the page the cat is on. Or ask her to name what's on each page.

Variation

Take close-up photos of your baby, other family members, a favorite stuffed animal, or other objects familiar to your baby. Paste them into another book.

46. Pail Pal

Reason for Toy

Research has shown that the older baby cherishes a collection of small objects. Here's a container for them. The pail, when empty, also serves as a plaything to carry around or swing and swat against solid pieces of furniture.

Materials

1 large Clorox bottle, very well washed
3 colorful strips of fabric
sandpaper

Instructions

1. Cut off Clorox container top with sharp scissors, making it about 5½" high. Sand edge if it feels at all ragged or sharp.
2. With pinking shears cut 3 different colored fabric strips about 1¾" × 20". Fold the fabric strips in half lengthwise and braid them together.
3. Cut a hole in 2 sides of the container near the top. With scissors poke an end of the braid through each hole from outside toward inside. Tie 2 large knots in braid ends on inside to make handle.

How to Use

Fill pail with 5 or 6 kitchen utensils or household odds and ends (See next pattern, Collector's Items, and the Serendipity List at the end of the book.)

Variation

Use a large round cookie or cracker tin in addition to the pail above. The cylindrical shape is a good one, and your baby will like the shine of the metal inside. When he peers in he'll see a bit of himself and the toys reflected. You could cover this container with patterned Con-Tact paper or leave it as is.

Your child's third container for small objects could be a basket or plastic food storage box. Fill each container with toys or household items and keep each in a different room.

47. Collector's Items

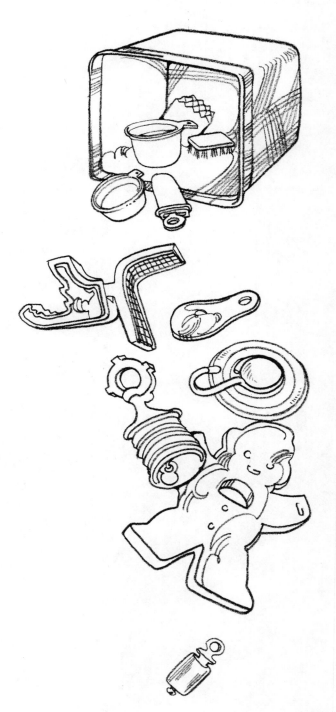

Reason for Toy

The interestingly shaped items listed here will fill the containers mentioned under Pail Pal, the previous pattern. Babies adore playing with small objects. They enjoy both an exploration type of experience and a mastery one with them. In exploration experiences, they examine objects to determine their characteristics. This involves behaviors such as mouthing the objects, striking them against something, and turning them around to see all sides of them. In mastery experiences, they practice little skills on them such as nesting, stacking, fitting, standing up, or rolling them.

Materials

Toys:

commercial ones or those made from patterns in this book (for example, Tube Twins, Egg-Rolling Contest, Sound Experiment (see Chapter Six)

Kitchen gadgets:

tea infuser, melon baller, rubber spatula, small strainer, small funnel, plastic cookie cutter, bottle stopper, egg separator

Household Objets d'Art:

roll of masking tape, toothbrush, key ring, soap dish, stamp dispenser, clothespins, plastic bathroom drinking cup, tub or sink stopper (rubber disk style), napkin rings

Wastebasket finds:

cardboard boxes, pieces of junk mail, shirt cardboard, rubber glove (cleansed of any detergent), empty typewriter reel, colorful plastic tops to spray cans

How to Use

Remembering your baby's interest in small objects, be alert to notice those that are in your own house and in the home of relatives and friends. When you spot a curiously contoured or textured item (if it is safe and unbreakable), share it with your toddler for a few moments. If you are in your own home, let her borrow it for her collection. If you are in a relative's or friend's house and the object is to be disposed of, ask if you can keep it for your toddler.

Variations

For additional ideas, turn to the Serendipity List at the back of this book. You may wish to keep adding to your collector's treasures. Thirty or 40 items are not considered unreasonable according to toddler observers. You may prefer to keep the number down because of clutter. If so, then rotate her supply by putting away those objects she's tired of and providing fresh ones.

Safety Note

Make sure the things you choose have no rough edges or sharp points and no hinged areas where fingers could get pinched. Does any part screw off? Don't use it. If there's a question, supervise play.

48. First Puzzle

Reason for Toy

For toddlers, a favorite form of work (sometimes called play by adults) is fitting one object to another. This will be accomplished here with little pain, and therefore much pleasure. Both the circle and frame are satisfying objects simply to tote about the house.

Materials

corrugated cardboard, about ¼" thick, cut from sturdy carton
white typing paper
red and green felt-tip pens (and other colors, if you wish)
transparent Con-Tact paper
red and green cloth tape, 1½" wide
Elmer's Glue-All

Instructions

1. Cut two 9" x 9" squares from cardboard carton. A sharp mat knife works well.
2. From the middle of each square, in exactly the same place, cut a circle 5" in diameter (a).
3. Trim all the way around the hole, shaving off another ⅛" of cardboard to make the hole 5¼" in diameter.
4. With plenty of glue, laminate the 2 squares and the 2 circles together.
5. Glue white paper to one side of the circle and one side of the square.
6. With felt-tip pens, draw a face on the white side of the circle (any colors) and red diagonal stripes on the square.
7. Cut out 4 pieces of Con-Tact paper to match both shapes and cover both sides of the cardboard pieces.
8. Bind edges of square with green tape.

9. Bind face with green and the hole with red. To bind edges of face and hole, snip the tape ½" deep every ¾" on both sides. This creates a tab effect (b). Lay the tape centered on the circumference of each circle and press the tabs around the hole and the face on both front and back sides. The face should fit very easily into the hole.

How to Use

Let a baby less than 1 year old simply play with the face as a hand toy, talking to it or carrying it around. He may peek coyly at you through the hole in the frame. The older baby will be more interested in the hole as a place where the puzzle piece belongs.

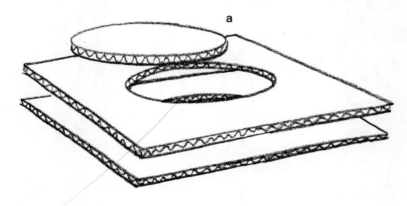

a

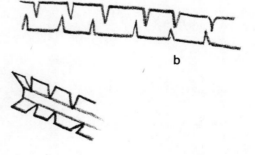

b

49. Nesting Rings

Reason for Toy

Fiddling with these rings gives your baby something to do when she's standing in the crib—at least, until her legs give way from exhaustion!

Babies like to see objects change in shape. These rings keep altering in appearance when handled. They cluster together, sliding inside each other, or spread out in a colorful row.

Materials

empty plastic orange juice can
empty toilet-paper roll
cylindrical oatmeal box
cylindrical salt box
cloth tape
Con-Tact paper, brightly colored or patterned, or pieces of bright
    fabric
Elmer's Glue-All
heavyweight string

Instructions

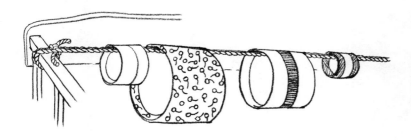

1. Cut 4 rings, about 2″ to 4″ wide, from containers of varying diameters.
2. Cover any rough edges with cloth tape.
3. Cover cardboard or plastic rings with Con-Tact paper or fabric. If you use fabric, cover rings with glue and then attach fabric, cut to size.

How to Use

Thread rings along string and tie ends to crib rail near footboard. Or move dowel to foot of crib and thread rings on dowel. When your baby starts pulling herself to a standing position, she can play with these as she stands or sidesteps around crib.

Variation

Thread a string through holes in the handles of a set of measuring cups. Stretching the string fairly taut, tie each end to crib rail.

50. Feed the Clown

Reason for Toy

Putting things into a container and then getting things out is a toddler's form of recreation with all the earmarks of a task. Fun for a baby is an activity that blends a sense of work and a sense of play.

Materials

cardboard box, not smaller than 4½″ x 6″, with hinge-style lid the flap of which tucks in easily
corrugated cardboard
white typing or drawing paper
felt-tip pens or crayons
transparent Con-Tact paper
Scotch transparent tape

Instructions

1. Cut the white paper the size of the box side. Draw a clown face as big as the paper itself, making an open grin about 2½″ wide and 1″ deep from upper to lower lip.
2. Lay drawing on side of box. Tape to hold it in place. Cut open the mouth, cutting through both paper and box lid.
3. Cover the top, sides, and bottom of the box with Con-Tact paper. (Cover so that you can still open box and retrieve things dropped inside.)
4. Slit Con-Tact paper over the mouth and fold to inside (a).
5. Make corrugated cardboard "cookies" (circles) to feed clown, or feed him real cookies or crackers.

How to Use

Holes exist to poke things into, a toddler thinks. When you point to the clown's mouth and say, "Give the man a cookie," your toddler will gleefully comply. Offer him help in opening the box to retrieve the cookies until he can do it himself.

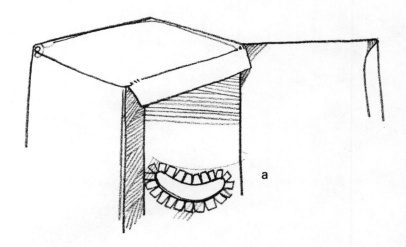

a

51. Stacking and Nesting

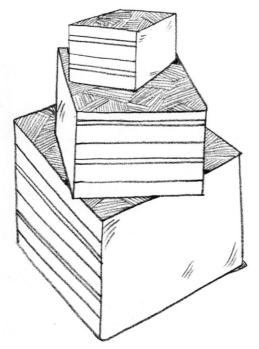

Reason for Toy

Seriated materials teach a child about sequential order. Lining these up and stacking or nesting them builds concepts that are the foundations of mathematics. Color-matching can also be practiced with these toys.

Set of Milk Cartons

Materials

gallon, halfgallon, and quart milk cartons
pieces of striped and solid fabric
Elmer's Glue-All

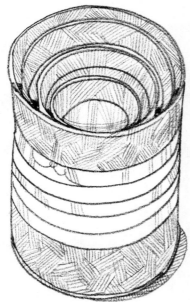

Instructions

1. Cut off the quart carton 3″ from the bottom to form a 3″ cube. Cut off the half gallon 4¾″ from the bottom to make a 4¾″ cube, and cut off the gallon to make a 5½″ cube.
2. Cut 2 pieces of striped fabric 3″ x 4″ and 2 pieces of solid fabric also 3″ x 4″.
3. Smear a liberal layer of glue all over 2 opposite sides of the quart cube and 1″ down into inside. Adhere striped fabric, folding extra inch inside.
4. Smear glue on other 2 sides, and adhere plain fabric. Opposite sides of the cube should match in color.
5. Cut both fabrics to fit the half-gallon carton and adhere the matching fabrics to opposite sides of the cube.
6. Cut both fabrics to fit the gallon carton and adhere the matching fabrics to opposite sides of the cube.
7. Use one of the fabrics or a new one to cover the bottoms of the cartons (optional).

Set of Cans

Materials

several tin cans of various diameters (1-pound coffee can, fruit,
    soup, tomato paste, etc.)
cloth tape, at least 1½" wide, in 2 colors and possibly 2 widths

Instructions

1. Remove one end of each can.
2. Hammer down any place where metal sticks out on inside
   rim.
3. Soak off labels.
4. Cover rims with cloth tape.
5. With more cloth tape and alternating colors, make stripes on
   the outsides of the cans. Leave ¼" to ½" of shiny metal
   showing between stripes to catch the light.

How to Use

You can let your child teach herself how to stack or nest these
cans and cartons in the correct order through handling them
over a period of time. If she seems to want guidance, you can
respond to her efforts with enthusiastic comments like "Aah!
That fits," or disappointed shakes of the head, "No, that doesn't."
Use the number of cans that seem appropriate to her ability
level.

   After your child has learned to nest the milk cartons in correct
order, call her attention to the plain sides and the striped sides.
Suggest she nest them so that the plain sides are next to each
other.

52. Crawler's Tunnel and Cruiser's Trail

Reason for Toy

Crawling is more fun for a baby when he has an interesting enclosure to enter, investigate, hide in, peer out of, and leave behind in a flash of swiftly moving limbs. Cruising, the pre-walker's style of negotiating space by sidestepping, is more fun when he can meander along a winding pathway.

Materials

several strong cardboard cartons, about 18″ high (from rear of stores in shopping center)
1 large carton, 2″ x 2″ x 2″
piece of fabric, brightly patterned or colored
pictures cut from magazines or coloring books
transparent Con-Tact paper
Elmer's Glue-All

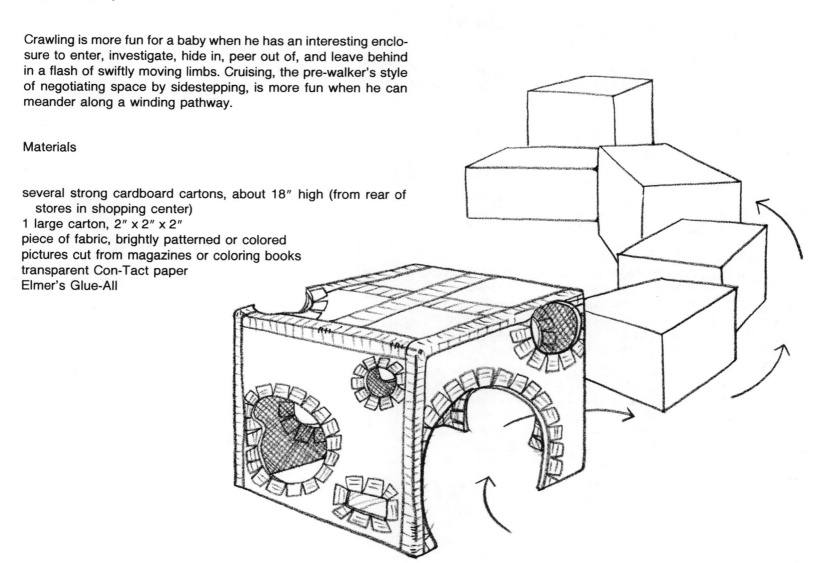

Instructions

1. With a mat knife cut off top flaps of 2'-square carton. Turning it upside down, cut a couple of free-form "doors" on adjoining sides.
2. Carve out some free-form windows and a peep hole in low and high positions on the walls and ceiling.
3. Cut with pinking shears several 4"-wide strips of fabric. (When applied, these will reinforce the box, pad the cut edges a little, and jazz up the appearance.)
4. Applying glue liberally, adhere strips of fabric to all seams on the box and to all edges. Also glue fabric strips around all door and window openings, slitting them at intervals about 1" apart so they will go around curves.
5. Glue a few pictures on the inside walls. Protect them with a layer of Con-Tact paper.

How to Use

If your baby is crawling only and not pulling himself up to a standing position yet, place just the decorated tunnel in the playroom or yard. If he is pulling to stand and ready to start sidestepping along the crib rail or coffee table, arrange a trail of cartons turned upside down. Resting his hands firmly on the tops of these boxes, he can wend his way along from one to the other. Rearrange the cartons occasionally to vary his route, sometimes beginning, sometimes ending with the tunnel.

53. Smokestack

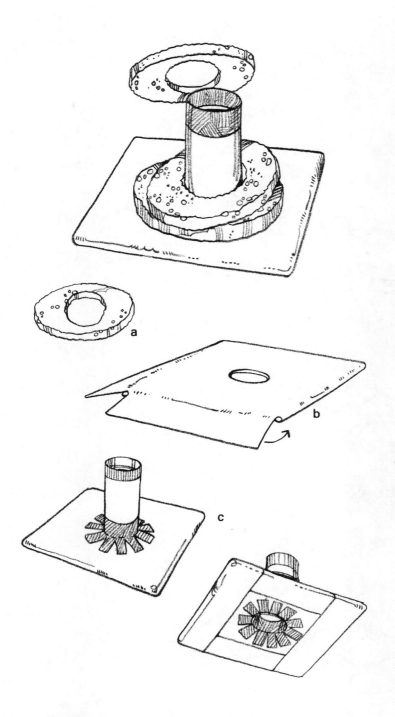

Reason for Toy

Fitting the sponge rings onto the roll and sliding them down presents the kind of challenge a toddler welcomes. Performing simple feats with objects now becomes more interesting than just examining them.

Materials

3 colored round or oval kitchen sponges, 4″ in diameter
1 empty toilet-paper roll
a 6″ square of corrugated cardboard, cut from a carton
cloth tape, 1½″ wide
colored Con-Tact paper

Instructions

1. Wash sponges well until tasteless. (You can put in machine with laundry.)
2. Cut a hole 2″ in diameter in each sponge (a).
3. Cover toilet-paper roll with Con-Tact paper and make a border of cloth tape around the top edge.
4. Cut a hole 2″ in diameter in center of cardboard.
5. Cover cardboard with Con-Tact paper, cutting out the center where the hole in the cardboard is (b).
6. Stick toilet-paper roll into hole. Attach it there with tape around bottom and top sides of cardboard. Slit tape to make it fit (c).

How to Use

Present this toy at a young enough age so that the job of fitting the rings to the roll is difficult for your child. If she has already mastered this type of task, the toy will quickly bore her.

Chapter Six

14 to 24 Months: Play—The Work of Toddlerhood

EDUCATION

Toddlers put in a full day of "work" when they play all day with toys. They are meeting challenges with them. They are learning from them. They are achieving through involvement with them. They approach play much as adults approach a job. Understanding play materials and figuring out things to do with them is your offspring's daily business.

The months before 2 years, though, are also a time toddlers want to get to know their parents better. Your child needs periods of your undivided attention and exchanges of affection and conversation more than ever.

Sound education now depends largely on achieving a proper balance between your toddler's interest in you and his interest in the world around him. Well-developing children have a very positive relationship with the parent that looks after them, but they do not cling to that person most of the day. Their increasing interest in their primary caregiver is balanced by continued curiosity about their environment and the things in it. To avoid having a clinging 2-year-old, be sure you are making the physical environment around him rich enough. Then it will frequently attract your toddler to become occupied with it.

Comfortable easy socializing with you often is desirable. The span of time from 14 to 24 months may be more crucial to the development of a good relationship with your child than any other period in your interwoven lifetimes. You should be sure you are not overscheduled with professional or volunteer activities outside, or even inside, the home during this year. However, you can make interesting objects and activities available to engage your child's attention and involve him in independent play for many intervals during the day. If you are working, you can teach the caregiver the educational value of such materials and activities.

Another way to balance a toddler's tendency to over-concentrate on the parent or the full-time caregiver is to give him all sorts of opportunities to practice his newest gross-motor skills. If your son has just mastered the art of walking, give him a variety of places to go walking on. What surfaces are available to walk on? Carpet, floor, grass, dirt road, woodsy trail, sidewalk, boardwalk? A change of surface can stimulate interest in the pastime of walking, making even more of a game out of it. A trip to the bank or the spacious lobby of an office building offers the chance to walk on smoothly polished tiles, perhaps with a bold checkerboard pattern. Challenges that might make strolling more interesting for the sturdy walker are a field with tall grass or a slanted surface such as a ramp for the handicapped leading into a public building.

As concerned as you are with your child's early education, you may have to watch that you don't overdo the teaching aspect of your role. Don't make a captive of your child in order to teach him something. For instance, don't make him sit longer with you looking at a book than he wants to. Instead take your cues from him. Observe what activities he is drawn to and focus any teaching remarks on that toy or activity.

One of the ways a child is commonly held captive is in a car seat. Just when your son is itchy to be physically active, he may be forced by circumstances into a long drive; a half hour is a long time to a toddler. There are several ways you can make this imprisoning situation more educational. Try singing to your child. (Borrow a library book on folk tunes and traditional children's songs and bone up.) Or sing some of the popular songs on the radio. Listening to your rendition would be far more beneficial for your child than hearing the recording artist.

Do you know any nursery rhymes? Reciting these can keep a child content in a car seat for quite a while. Some nursery rhymes have finger movements that can accompany them. (A book on finger rhymes will illustrate these movements.) You can teach these rhymes to your child at home. Then, in the car, you can say the rhyme and he can accompany you with finger movements (your hands remaining on the wheel!).

The education of your baby flourishes during this stage if you continue to encourage his exploring and approve his examining. Your vigilance has to be intensified, though, because nimble climbing means a toddler can suddenly arrive at heights from which it would be harmful to fall. Also, the poisonous cleaning products or medicines you once may have moved from low to high places may now have to be kept behind hard-to-open or locked doors.

To satisfy your baby's lively curiosity, you may want to give him access to more rooms than you have so far. Porch, patio, or deck can make great play areas when accident-proofed. A garage can come in handy for investigating, under supervision, on a rainy day. If you spend a lot of time in the kitchen or laundry room, try to design these spaces as "amusement parks" for the under-2 set. In the following pages, you will find some ideas on how to do this. A splash area for water play would be a good feature. Or our plan for a Paper Corner may spark your imagination.

Introduce your child to environments other than his home at this time. Keep an eye out around your town or city for intriguing settings. For example, explore shallow steps up to the Post Office; visit a park with a fountain; or walk along various pathways of brick, pine chips, or slate. Shopping malls or parks sometimes have nice low benches for climbing on. Outdoor sculptures may have niches to crawl into or arches to scamper under.

The growth of intelligence is closely linked to familiarity with language. Talk frequently to your youngster, well before he talks back to you. During the day your child will bring to you objects he finds on his excursions away from your side. Don't be indifferent to his finds, lost in thought, or engrossed in conversation. Take a few seconds to remark on these with enthusiasm (unless they are "no-no's"). Label his discoveries. Describe them in words he can understand or guess at. Call attention to a detail about them he might not notice. For example, "Hey! You found a clam-shell. Feel it. It's rough on the outside, smooth on the inside. See, it's got a little purple place inside in the center."

Educating your baby at this stage can mean pointing out similarities and differences between objects. "This shell and this stone are both white. But the shell is light and the stone is heavy." You can mention interesting peculiarities. "Here's a stone that has some dirt stuck to it."

Such exchanges not only sharpen the toddler's powers of observation but help his language comprehension. He learns more words when a conversation is one-on-one with him. How-ever, also give him opportunities to hear you and your husband talking or you and a sibling.

"Reading" picture books often means skipping a mediocre text and simply pointing to and labeling the pictures, emphasizing things that are familiar to your child and perhaps explaining those that are not.

Now 1½-year-olds start to feel the emotion known as pride, and praise for your child's mini-accomplishments means a lot. You foster the ability to feel pride when you praise him for a clever achievement such as a high armchair climbed or a box pried open. You can empathize with his signs of pride by warm verbal approval, clapping your hands, cheering, or simply smiling or hugging.

Nothing succeeds like success. Self-esteem burgeons when a toddler feels his efforts are successful. You can set the stage for success by providing simple problems you know he can solve. Offer 2 different lids and 1 pot; ask him to put the right lid on the pot. Hand him forks to store in the right compartment of a silverware drawer. Other matching games can be played with the simplest puzzles (included in this chapter) and a set of beginner lotto cards. Doing these puzzles means fitting a shape to a cut-out hole. Lotto involves matching identical picture cards to illustrations on a game board. (Lotto, usually sold as a game for kindergarteners, does not have to be played as a game.) When your child is ready for these activities, look up patterns in this chapter called Can Challenges, Second Puzzle, Size Trials, and Lotto.

BEHAVIORS

Your child becomes an increasingly stable walker during this pe-riod. Soon she discovers running and it seems as though she wants to run everywhere and never slow down to a walk again. She becomes increasingly adept at climbing, which places a greater demand on you for alertness as to her whereabouts. A toddler can become quite coordinated in maneuvering a little 4-wheeled cart designed in the shape of an animal or perhaps a fire engine. She straddles it, sits on a seat, and walks it forward.

If you wish to encourage these gross-motor skills, introduce your toddler to other kids in the park, playground, or day-care center. Observation of peers having fun is a strong incentive to develop such skills. Your toddler may even feel a primitive form of competitiveness.

Even though it may seem to you that your child is the personi-fication of perpetual motion, in fact she isn't always on the move. Most toddlers stand still or sit still and stare a good fifth of their waking hours. In fact, staring is their single most time-consuming activity. They stare at a toy, a parent at work, another child, or some happening nearby.

Another characteristic behavior of this period is seeking out the parent. Your toddler will re-establish contact often during the day, looking for comfort if hurt, assistance if frustrated, or approval if pleased with herself or some object. An innate desire simply to socialize also brings her to your side. Ankle-grabbers, skirt-tuggers, and knee-ticklers are some of the epithets children have won because of their tendency to cling to Mom or Dad or else, having sallied forth, to return often to home base for reas-surance.

Well-developing children are not without a sense of humor at this age. Parents' antics can make them laugh, and they, in turn, will clown in order to provoke your laughter. Chasing and catching a toddler and then letting go can produce the giggles. Or perhaps hiding yourself behind a tree and letting yourself be found will evoke hilarity. Kids will throw a ball wildly or make a stuffed animal do tricks in an effort to get you to laugh (or feign laughter). Kids can be crowd-pleasers. They love a good audi-ence. All toss, tickle, nuzzle, and kiss games also have good humor value.

Games with a surprise factor may tickle your child's funny bone. Try hiding something in your fist, a lipstick perhaps. Let her pry open your fingers one at a time to find the treasure. After doing this several times, surreptitiously slip in a bottle stop-per instead of the lipstick. The next uncurling of your fingers will reveal a surprise. Expect a smile and a request to repeat the game *ad infinitum*.

Even though you may have done a model job of child-rearing up until 14 months, you may suddenly encounter outbursts of negativeness in your child. The smoothness of your past rapport makes you feel totally unprepared for and baffled by this ruffling of the waters. There may be tough moments for you, wondering how best to deal with lack of cooperation, resistance to your requests, and stubborn opposition to your wishes. You may mourn that total innocence of the first year and fear this outcropping of guile.

Looking at this interpersonal tension in as generous a light as possible, you can see it as the development of autonomy. Your toddler becomes aware at this stage that she has a selfhood apart from your selfhood. And with this awareness comes a desire for independence or self-government. If you understand what's going on, you can put up with some petulant *no*'s without feeling hurt, annoyed, or wanting to punish harshly. Rather than feeling these flickers of rebellion must be stamped out, you can recognize that you are bearing witness to a maturing process. Your child wants some authority over her own life. She wants to share in decisions such as what she wears in the morning or when she gets undressed at night. When possible, give her choices between 2 things both of which you approve of. Modify the environment so she is able to do more things for herself. Your infant is becoming a person. Together you are starting to work out a harmonious relationship between 2 individuals in a family. This relationship is one you will be molding for the rest of your lives.

This period of negativeness usually lasts about 6 months and, near the second birthday, a natural harmony between parent and child is usually restored. But it is restored on a new basis with each family member recognizing that the other is an individual, having a measure of self-government.

During the troubled period, a parent need never spoil the child, permit temper tantrums, nor abdicate the right to a final say. However, you can let your child have her way occasionally when you're not in a hurry, when there's no personal danger involved, or when the controversy is over an unimportant issue. Then she will feel your respect for her as an individual, and she will get some practice at independence.

If you feel secure, it will not bother you if your child doesn't always behave as if she adores you. You can tolerate some opposition without feeling you are spoiling her or letting her take advantage of you. On the other hand, you can hold your ground and assert your will when it is not a whim but a decision based on sound judgment about what is right and proper for that particular moment on that particular day. Cheerful firmness works well during a clash of wills. Also, a little imaginative effort to change the mood and move on to less controversial activities helps a lot.

ABILITIES

By the age of 2, well-developing children possess half a dozen or so social skills and an equal number of cognitive skills. They surface gradually between 8 and 24 months of age. Additional basic social and cognitive skills emerge in the third year of life.

These specific abilities, common to all nicely advancing 2-year-olds, have been identified by a Harvard team of educational researchers. The following is their list of the abilities usually exhibited by above-average 2-year-olds. These abilities and a few more advanced ones are fully described in Burton L. White's book, *The First Three Years of Life*.

Social Abilities

Getting and holding the attention of adults
Using adults as resources after first determining that a job is too difficult
Expressing affection to adults
Expressing mild annoyance to adults
Showing pride in personal accomplishment
Engaging in role play or make-believe activities

Cognitive Abilities

Good language development
Noticing small details or discrepancies
Anticipating consequences
Dealing with abstractions
Using resources effectively
Maintaining concentration on a task while simultaneously keeping track of what is going on around one in a fairly busy situation (dual focusing)

During this exciting period in your child's life, you will probably be awestruck by the growth in his understanding and use of language. By 2, he will have a vocabulary of hundreds of words at his disposal for conversation. He will be able to repeat new words you suggest as soon as you say them. He will have figured out grammatical rules well enough to make use of plurals, negatives, and prepositions when he talks. He will be able to understand instructions, warnings, and prohibitions. This will be helpful as you try to impart the rules that are to govern your tot's conduct. He will enjoy holding a conversation sometimes short, sometimes long, for various reasons: for a serious purpose (about a task he wants to accomplish), just for fun, to keep your attention focused on him, or to act out a pretend game.

Language gives your toddler such pleasure at this stage that he will sit still awhile to listen to a story told or read, or to hear nursery rhymes and poems. Poems can be very satisfying, partly because they are short and partly because of the elements of rhyme and rhythm which they embody.

Some children can identify letters and numbers before the age of 2 if those presented are large enough. They need to be 2 to 3 inches high. An alphabet of 3-dimensional letters enables you to play games that teach a child to recognize the various shapes. You can say, "Here is A. Go hide A under the sofa." Then when your child has done this, you can whimper, "Oh, dear, we've lost A. Where is A?" The child will merrily retrieve it. You can make the hide-and-seek game more complicated as the child learns several letters. He will then have to pick A out from a small group of other letters.

Children nearing 2 years have also learned to read words by sight, not by the phonic method, with 2- to 3-inch-high letters. You can buy or make word cards with letters this size. Print *Mommy, Daddy,* your dog's name, your child's name for his grandmother, and other words that label things important to your child. Your child will memorize the shape of the word and associate it with the name or word you pronounce when you show the card. Make a cheerful game of presenting these words and allow the session to last only a minute or so.

Teaching letters or words at this tender age is not necessary to intellectual development. It's an activity to engage in only if it's fun for both you and your child. Don't make such a session the least bit tedious; keep it light. But unless you continue with the learning, your child will forget the words he once knew.

The effect of such lessons on a child is usually to notice that words are everywhere: on the sides of buildings, on billboards, on signs, and on packages in the supermarket. He may ask relentlessly for your rendition of many words he sees.

A real ability to think becomes noticeable in the few months before your child's second birthday. One meaning of the word *think* is to turn over ideas and images in the mind. A baby who moves about the house conscious only of the places, things, or people in front of his eyes has not reached the "think" stage yet. Anything out of sight is out of mind. Gradually a toddler begins to get liberated from a total confinement to the concrete. Memory develops, and he sees things in his mind (as images or ideas) that are not necessarily in front of him.

Until this dawning of the thinking process, a baby works out little problems physically. For instance, to fit a shape into a shape-sorting box, he keeps trying holes until the shape drops in. He doesn't look at each hole and think about which one matches his shape. Near 2 years, he begins to be able to figure things out in his mind, making a shrewd estimate as to the correct hole before trying it.

You can tell when the mental wheels are turning. You see your child pause just before acting. You can feel him contemplating what move he's going to make. He might be going over the alternative courses of action concerning the ball he's playing with. "Shall I roll the ball down the hill? Shall I throw it to Daddy? Or shall I keep it and run away?" Suddenly he sprints.

Soon he may size up a task inwardly, decide he can't do it, and ask for help. It's no good saying, "You haven't tried," because in his mind he has tried.

INTERESTS

The 14- to 24-month-old has a wide variety of interests. Here are descriptions of key ones and some suggestions on how to play up to them.

One of the great interests of this age is that most fundamental of substances: water. Water behaves in such a variety of ways; it gushes, trickles, patters, and ripples. Let your toddler play with it in the bathtub, in the bathroom or kitchen sink, and in a dishpan or bucket on the kitchen floor. You can add to her collection of bath toys which you made or accumulated during the previous stage of development. New types of containers with odd outlets channel water in ways that capture your baby's attention.

If the weather is good, time spent with a hose or outdoor

faucet or backyard kiddie pool can be immensely interesting. Your surveillance near the pool is essential.

Water play is not only fascinating but also therapeutic. Some mothers save the opportunity to play with water for that time of day when their child is most tired and therefore likely to be fussy or for a time when they are busiest and can't play with the child but can still keep an eye on her for safety reasons.

Field trips away from home to look at water or possibly play with it should be arranged. If you live in the city, plan excursions to plaza fountains, a drinking fountain in an office building, an architect's indoor or outdoor reflecting pool, or a wishing pool where people toss in pennies. If you live in the country, plan outings to a brook, pond, waterfall, or lakeside beach or seashore. Whenever possible give the child a chance to interact with the water by wading, splashing, throwing in sticks or pebbles, floating toy boats, or filling paper cups or pails with water and then pouring it out.

Another basic substance, not quite as cheap as water, is paper. Think of all the kinds of paper you have in the house: tissue paper, toilet paper, face tissues, wax paper, newspapers, magazines, junk mail, discarded envelopes. All these are potential toys. They can provide amusement for relatively long periods of time on the proverbial rainy day.

Also make use of paper products such as cardboard or corrugated boxes. Any household accumulates all kinds of boxes: shoe boxes, gift boxes, boxes that toothpaste and cosmetics are packaged in, detergent boxes, and bakery folding boxes.

Another paper product is a book. The book with stiff pages is still best at this age. Not only does a toddler still enjoy a book as a hinged object, but she can be rough with such a book and not risk tearing its pages. Make or select books with objects recognizable to her rather than illustrations of things she hasn't seen or could never see (such as a rabbit dressed up in clothes). Fantasy stories will be more appropriate for a child older than 2. Our Activity Book calls for finger involvement with each page.

A strong interest at this age is junior–size gymnastic equipment. Your furniture becomes climbing apparatus. This chapter includes a pattern called Balance Beam. And you might want to build or buy a mini–jungle gym and small slide. Recreational centers now hold gym classes for toddlers in some areas.

Another known interest of the under–2-year-old is the ball. It can be any kind of ball: a football, a beach ball, a tennis ball, a rubber ball, a Ping-Pong ball. The latter has particular fascination

because when thrown onto a bare floor, it produces syncopated taps pleasant to the ear and it bounces in erratic patterns interesting to the eye. Balls are satisfactory to toddlers because they provide a good reason to enjoy or show off their running skills. They can run after the ball they throw. The chase and the retrieval become tasks that can be accomplished or problems that can be solved. Success usually elicits praise from the caregivers, so play with a ball brings a toddler the same satisfaction that work brings an adult.

Another reason a toddler likes a ball is that it helps her entice a sibling or parent to play with her. Few can resist an invitation to play catch. Our Ball Bag provides a way to store the balls or tote them to Grandpa's house.

Dolls are a surefire success with toddlers, boys as well as girls, of course. Just before a new baby arrives at the house is a logical time for the purchase of a baby doll. Otherwise toddlers like the resemblance to themselves suggested by a realistic child-like doll. They enjoy imitating with the doll the maternal and paternal care that they are receiving from their parents. It gives them a chance to imitate grown-up behavior. Such imitation makes them feel bigger and more important.

Doll carriages get a lot of attention too. Toddlers are still being pushed in a stroller, so they like imitating the way you push them. Also, the wheels on the bottom of the carriage are innately attractive as a toy in and of themselves. Turn the carriage upside down so your child can spin the wheels freely.

Almost every toddler goes through a stage where you'd swear she's a born mechanic. She loves fiddling with locks, door handles, gate latches; window hardware; the wheels of her wagon, walker, or doll carriage; and the pedals of her brother's or sister's tricycle. You might go to the local hardware store or builders' supply outlet and see what sort of safe, real-life objects you could turn into toys. Remember that they should be at least 1¼ inches in diameter and 2¼ inches deep, with no sharp points or edges. Make sure any interlocking pieces come apart easily enough so your toddler doesn't get frustrated and check also that the individual parts are big enough not to be swallowed. Our pattern for a Mechanism Board may turn out to be your child's all-time favorite.

As in the previous stage, children approaching 2 years like to be the cause of a dramatic effect. They are extremely delighted when they can move a switch which activates a machine producing sound, light, or changing visual patterns. A cheap tape recorder could go a long way toward satisfying this inclination. Also, a child's record player—designed for abuse—could give your toddler a lot of pleasure, particularly if she is able to work the on-off mechanism herself.

Between 1 and 2 years of age is the heyday for containers and an abundance of small objects to go inside them. Your toddler will like all kinds of containers: narrow, wide, shallow, deep, round, square, and rectangular. They can be made of cardboard, plastic, metal, or wood. Think big—an angel food cake pan. Think small—a plastic soap dish. It would be fun if several had lids.

Little kids show their continuing interest in small portable objects in 2 ways: by examining them to understand their attributes, and by practicing simple skills on them to show their control over them. As your child nears 2 years an increasing amount of playtime is spent on the second type of activity. She'll throw balls, and she'll open and close boxes, jars, and drawers. She'll place things upright and knock them down. She'll take apart a toy and try to put it back together. She'll slip objects through openings and pour materials into and out of containers. She'll fit matching pieces together.

In spite of this strong focus on the phenomena of the physical world, your child is also showing more and more interest in you. This interest peaks at the age of 2. There is never a time in your child's life when your presence, your close relationship, and your intercommunication will be more important. If you are a working person, try for shorter work hours during this period or for more freedom after work to concentrate on your child. Weekends could be orchestrated so you are very much on the scene while your child is awake.

Don't listen to put-downs of parenthood at this stage. Stick with friends and advisers who have strong maternal and paternal instincts and are proud of them. Time spent with your child now and careful attention to her needs will generate such good development that you will probably be freer later on than those parents who shortchange their child at this crucial period. Your child later will be more independent and problem-free, enabling you to pursue activities other than family care much of the day.

If you are bored with your child, your manner could soon warp your child's ways of getting and holding attention. If you are sincerely fascinated with her development, your manner is bound to build self-esteem in your offspring and thus encourage a positive style of social interaction. This fascination or appreciation of the miracle of human development is the name of the game. It usually guarantees success at child-rearing.

The toys described on the following pages do not have to be given in any special order. They are not sequenced exactly according to an assumed ability scale. However, in general, those requiring more advanced cognitive skills are placed toward the end of the chapter. Presenting these toys and noting your toddler's reactions to them will keep you attuned to her physical and mental progress.

Thumb through the pages and first make those patterns which you feel sure would appeal to your child. Toys are a magic means of bringing parent and child together. You may enjoy each other's company more when you explore a toy side by side. Watching your toddler work-play with them and occasionally joining in the fun will help make this stage of child-rearing one of the most entertaining and interesting experiences of your life.

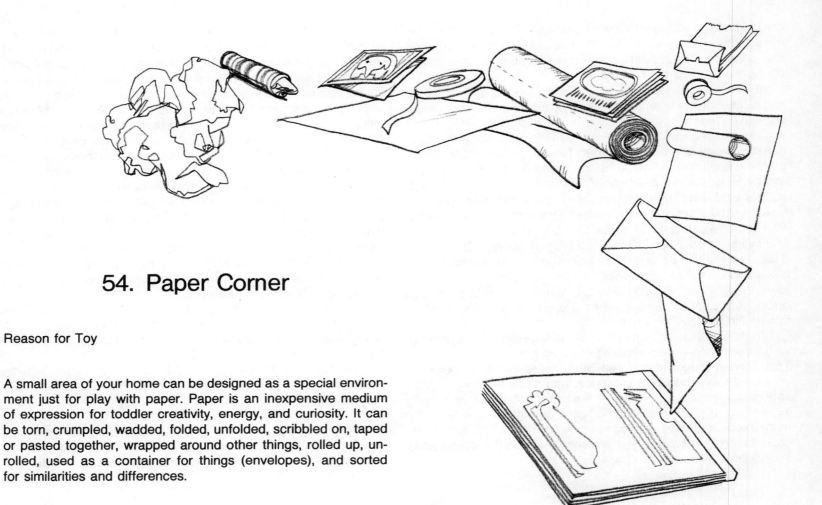

54. Paper Corner

Reason for Toy

A small area of your home can be designed as a special environment just for play with paper. Paper is an inexpensive medium of expression for toddler creativity, energy, and curiosity. It can be torn, crumpled, wadded, folded, unfolded, scribbled on, taped or pasted together, wrapped around other things, rolled up, unrolled, used as a container for things (envelopes), and sorted for similarities and differences.

Materials

1 roll of brown wrapping paper
some aluminum foil
paper towels and/or napkins
newspaper
white typing paper
colored construction paper
a pad of newsprint
used gift wrapping paper

old magazines
empty toilet-paper and paper-towel rolls
old greeting cards
paper bags
used envelopes in assorted sizes with flaps or without (trim them
  off)
some thick crayons
Scotch transparent tape
brightly colored cloth tape

Instructions

1. Designate an area for accumulating paper products. Provide a system of organizing and storing them, such as a set of cubbyholes, a bookcase, or closet shelves.
2. Hang the pad of newsprint low on the wall.
3. Assign some floor space nearby or a table or workbench for using the materials.

How to Use

A child will probably find ways of playing with the paper that the most ingenious adult could never think up. But inspire your child occasionally by picking out 2 or 3 types of paper goods and suggesting some way of combining them. For example, you could recommend he tape a greeting card to a sheet of newsprint and scribble a decoration all around it.

55. Activity Book

Reason for Toy

For active babies here's a picture book that offers activities to do rather than stories to listen to. Fidgety fingers can concentrate on things like stretching and snapping elastic, pretend hair-brushing, tucking in a baby, or untying a shoelace. This is the most complicated pattern in our book, but if you're handy with a sewing machine, a couple of evenings' efforts will produce a handsome and pleasing creation.

Materials

6 pieces of solid-color cloth, 20″ × 12″ (the 2 pieces used for the front and back covers could be different from the inner pages)
6 pieces of cardboard, 10¼″ × 8½″
fabric scraps: plain and flowered cotton, red and other color vinyl, fake fur, terrycloth, felt
4 large black buttons
polyester pillow stuffing
2 pieces of dress elastic, 6″ long (wide and narrow)
shoelace, 20″ to 22″ long
lightweight string, 8½″ long
1 or 2 cotton balls
plastic tube or heavy cord, about 11″ long
6 to 8 plumber's black rubber "O" rings, some 1″, others ¾″ in diameter
3 pieces of Velcro fastening, 1″ square, with matching halves
yarn (the color of your child's hair if possible)
thread
permanent felt-tip pens

Instructions

You are making a book of 12 cloth pages, including the covers, with cardboard inside each page to stiffen it. There will be a different activity for your baby on each page. First, you create

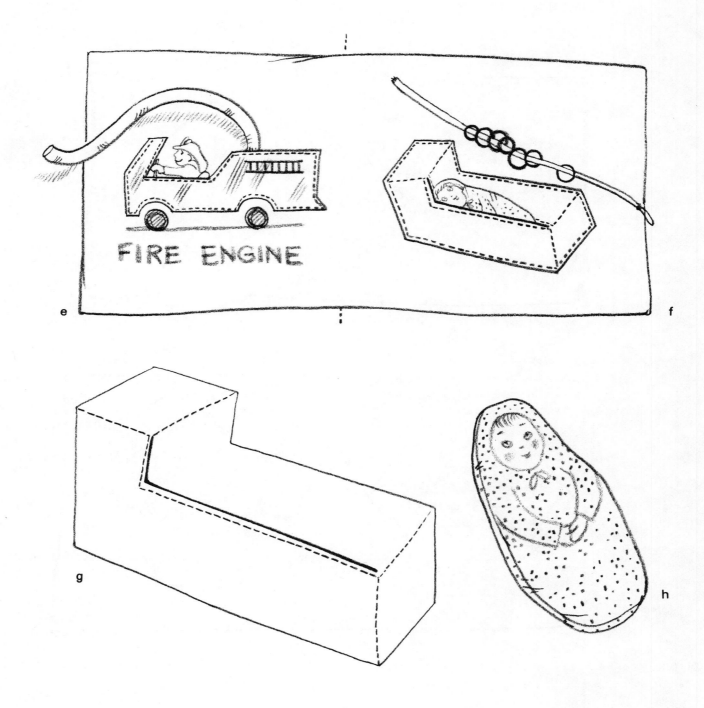

FIRE ENGINE

e

f

g

h

i

j

the activity for each page. Then you sew edges, insert cardboard, sew again, and then bind book together.

Lay out the pages. Each piece of fabric will be folded in half, making the front and back of each page. Start on the left-hand side of each piece of fabric.

Front Cover:

The cover page bears just the title *Book.*
1. Cut large block letters from 4 different scraps of flower-print cloth, each letter about 2½″ wide and 3″ tall.
2. Pin the letters to the left-hand side of your first piece of cloth, overlapping them a little.
3. Zigzag-stitch with a sewing machine around each letter, using a brightly colored thread (a).

Pages 1 and 2:

The next 2 facing pages will be elastic for your baby to pull on. (Try both hands at once pulling in opposite directions.)

1. On the right-hand side of your first piece of cloth, appliqué an arrow design cut from a fabric scrap about 8″ long.
2. Lay a piece of elastic on arrow and zigzag-stitch it in place in the middle (b).
3. Make the next page like this last one only have the arrow and elastic facing at right angles to the first one (c).

Page 3:

The next page is a child with lots of yarn hair. It can look like your baby or not. You can put a bow or a barrette in the hair or make it long and braid it.
1. On the cloth, draw the outlines of a simple face with felt-tip pens.
2. Lay a bunch of yarn (strands about 11″ long) from ear to ear across the top of the head. Using a zigzag stitch, sew through the whole wad once in the middle and once on each side (d).

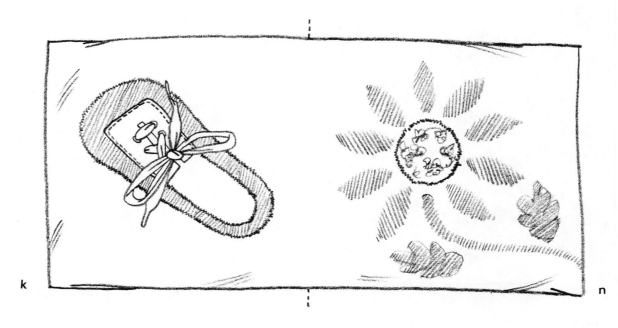

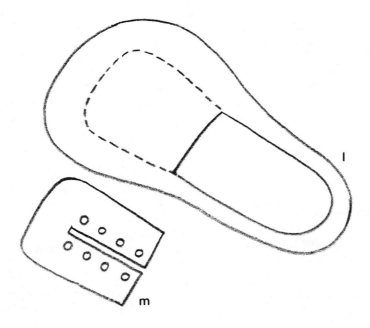

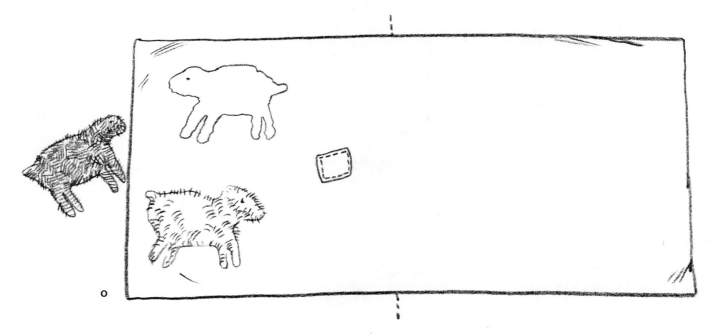

o

Page 4:

The facing page is a shiny fire engine (e).

1. Cut a fire engine shape out of red vinyl. Use a running stitch to sew it onto the cloth.
2. Sew on very securely large black buttons for wheels.
3. Use permanent felt-tip pens to draw a little firefighter, a ladder across the side of the engine, and the words *fire engine* below.
4. You can add a "fire hose" by sewing on at one end the length of heavy cord or plastic tube.

Page 5:

The next page has a baby doll which can be removed from its car bed. A mobile of rings which can be moved along a string hangs over the baby (f).

1. Cut out a car bed shape 6" long from felt. Slit it along solid line shown in figure (g).
2. Using contrasting thread and a running stitch, sew along dotted lines shown in figure (g).
3. Now stitch the bed onto the cloth page, using running stitch around perimeter of bed as shown in figure (f). Also stitch to page the inside of the bed above the slit where doll fits in.
4. To make a baby (h), cut 2 ovals about 3½" long from plain fabric.
5. On one draw a baby with felt-tip pen.
6. Put right sides together and stitch around edges, leaving an opening of 1½". Turn right sides out, lightly stuff, and hand-stitch opening closed.
7. Lay piece of string across page above bed. Zigzag-stitch it onto page across one end. Thread 6 or 8 plumber's rubber "O" rings onto string. Zigzag-stitch other end of string onto cloth (f).

Page 6:

The facing page is a rabbit with a fuzzy tail (i).

1. Draw the outline of a rabbit on the cloth with felt-tip pen.
2. Cut out a circle of white fake fur or use a ball of cotton for the tail. Hand-sew it securely in place.

Page 7:

The next page is a house with a door that opens and closes (j).
1. Draw or appliqué a house shape onto the cloth page. (If you appliqué a house shape, cut out square windows and door first.) With felt-tip pen, draw a person standing in the doorway.
2. Cut out a vinyl or felt door. Lay it over the person. Zigzag-stitch it in place along one side.

Page 8:

The facing page is a shoe to untie (k).
1. Cut a shoe shape, about 8¼" long and 3" wide, out of fabric (l).
2. Cut out a piece of vinyl 3¼" long. Slit it part way down the center and punch holes in it for shoelace (m).
3. Sew vinyl onto the shoe shape. Thread lace through the holes.
4. Appliqué entire shoe onto cloth page with zigzag stitch.

Page 9:

The next page is a flower to smell (n).
1. Draw a large flower onto the cloth page with felt-tip pens.
2. Cut out a circle of fabric about 2" in diameter for the center of the flower. Saturate a wad of cotton with perfume. Let it dry. Place it in center of flower and cover it with circle of fabric.
3. Zigzag-stitch the circle of fabric in place over the cotton.

Page 10:

This page is the inside of the back cover (o).
1. Sew pieces of Velcro on the cloth page.
2. Cut out 3 fake fur (or felt, corduroy, or terry) animal shapes and sew matching pieces of Velcro on the back of each one. The animals can be stuck to the page. Your baby can pull them off and restick them.

Back Cover:

To finish the book:

1. Turn all double pages right-side-in and sew along tops and bottoms (p).
2. Turn right-side out. Press if necessary.
3. Slip cardboard inside each page (q). The cardboard should be narrower than the page so there is a half inch or so of only cloth on the inner side of each page.
4. Fold in raw edges on inner side of each page, pin closed, and stitch. Through the cloth at the edge sew yarn in 2 places to tie pages together (r).

How to Use

Gather baby in your lap and have a cozy quiet time talking to her about each page. Watch her play with each picture and discover things to do with it. Don't hurry, and let her decide when to turn the page. You can name the parts of every picture.

Variations

The pages shown here are suggestions. There are many other possibilities for entertaining, educational pages for this or another activity book. A few recommendations are:
1. Felt hands with each finger numbered.
2. A zipper placed as the mouth of a big fish or on a pocket to hold a small object.
3. Artist's palette in felt with 4 "paint" circles—red, yellow, green, blue.
4. Half of a jacket front sewn to the page with a button sewn at the neck. Another half of a jacket with a buttonhole. The jacket is felt and the buttonhole just a slit.
5. On one page, a pocket holding 3 shapes of felt: triangle, circle, and square. On the facing page, outlines of the 3 shapes drawn with felt-tip pen. Large snaps can be sewn to the shapes and inside the outlines so shapes can be matched and snapped in place.
6. An animal appliquéd on the page. It can wear a ribbon belt or collar with a simple buckle that can be undone.

r

Smart Toys

56. Can Challenges

Reason for Toy

Playing with these cans exercises your baby's current ability to fit objects through openings. Gradually he recognizes differences in the size of objects and how to match the big object to the big opening.

Materials

2 tin cans with plastic lids (like coffee cans)
1 Ping-Pong ball
1 tennis ball

Instructions

1. Remove one end of one can and both ends of another.
2. Hammer down any sharp places left by can opener.
3. Cut a hole 2¾" in diameter in one plastic lid. Cut a hole 1¾" in diameter in other lid.
4. Put a lid on each can.

How to Use

Game I: Put lid with larger hole on can with open bottom. Let baby drop Ping-Pong ball in and fetch ball when it rolls out. Game II: Put lid with larger hole on can with bottom. Let baby drop Ping-Pong ball in and shake it out of opening. Game III: Try the first 2 games using lid with smaller hole. (Shaking the Ping-Pong ball out of smaller hole is hard to do.) Game IV: Introduce a tennis ball and present both cans with lids on. Your baby will notice it only fits through the larger opening.

57. Second Puzzle

Reason for Toy

A toddler is sensitive in a primitive way to her ability or failure to achieve. There'll be a gleam of pride in her eye when she fits puzzle pieces into their positions. Her pleasure will be enhanced if you are nearby and notice. She may show signs of frustration, such as throwing the pieces aside if you encourage her to fit them when she is not yet ready to enjoy such a task.

Materials

corregated cardboard, cut from sides of carton
cloth tape
Con-Tact paper, patterned and plain
Elmer's Glue-All

Instructions

1. With mat knife cut 2 cardboard rectangles 7" × 13". These will be your puzzle frames.
2. Cut out of one frame a square with 3½" sides and a triangle 3½" on each side.
3. Lay first frame with cut-outs on top of your other frame. Trace shapes through the holes and cut out another square and triangle.
4. Trim ⅛" off all sides of your puzzle pieces (so when bound with tape they still fit holes).
5. Glue (laminate) the 2 squares together, then the 2 triangles, and, finally, the 2 puzzle frames together.
6. Cover both sides of puzzle pieces with plain Con-Tact paper and cover both sides of frame with patterned Con-Tact paper.
7. Bind all edges with cloth tape.

How to Use

Let your child play with the frames and puzzle pieces however she wishes. Let her gradually discover that the pieces fit the holes. At first, the fit may occur by happenstance; later, it will be on purpose. If you're impatient for the discovery, demonstrate the fit once or twice, talking amiably about it. Then see if your child has a desire to imitate you.

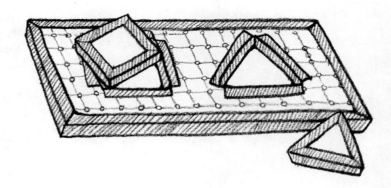

58. Picture Stowaways

Reason for Toy

Sliding things in and out of made-to-measure enclosures is a manual skill toddlers love exercising. The pictures stowed away inside these drawers are a happy discovery the first time and the many times thereafter.

Materials

large sliding box for wooden kitchen matches or similar box for
    cosmetic product (sturdier than match box)
3 small match boxes (optional)
pieces of bright fabric
picture or photo
transparent Con-Tact paper
Elmer's Glue-All

Instructions

1. Smear the whole outside of the box with glue and cover with a piece of fabric the dimensions of the box. When glue is dry, cover again with Con-Tact paper. (This process reinforces a box of flimsy cardboard.)
2. Smear the inside of the drawer with glue and cover with fabric to strengthen drawer.
3. Glue a photo or a picture on the bottom of the drawer and protect it with a layer of Con-Tact paper.

How to Use

The idea is to push the drawer part way out to peek at the picture. Instead, your child will probably push it all the way out at first.

He'll need help getting it back in. A variation in play is to let the toddler try another toy as a pushing tool, holding it and making it push the drawer forward. He could hide favorite toys inside. One day you could change the picture for a surprise when he opens the drawer.

    This toy doesn't stand up well to rough handling. Rather than leaving it in a container with other toys, keep it aside for moments when you are free to play with him.

Variation

Glue together 3 small match boxes, one on top of the other. Put a layer of glue on the sides where the striking strip is and cover with fabric. Put a layer of Con-Tact paper around the 3 boxes. Paste a little picture inside on the bottom of each drawer.

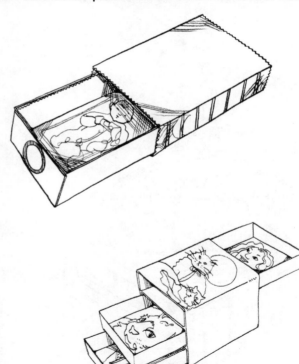

59. Early Stringing

Reason for Toy

Stringing beads onto a flexible string is a little too hard for the under-2 set. But stringing objects with generous holes in their middles onto a stiff, thick wire is an action near-2 toddlers can manage quite nicely.

Materials

small jewelry or gift box, about 3½" square and 1" deep, with separate lid
#10 automotive wire (stiff but bendable, covered with rubber, available at hardware store)
bright cloth tape
Con-Tact paper, plain or patterned (optional)

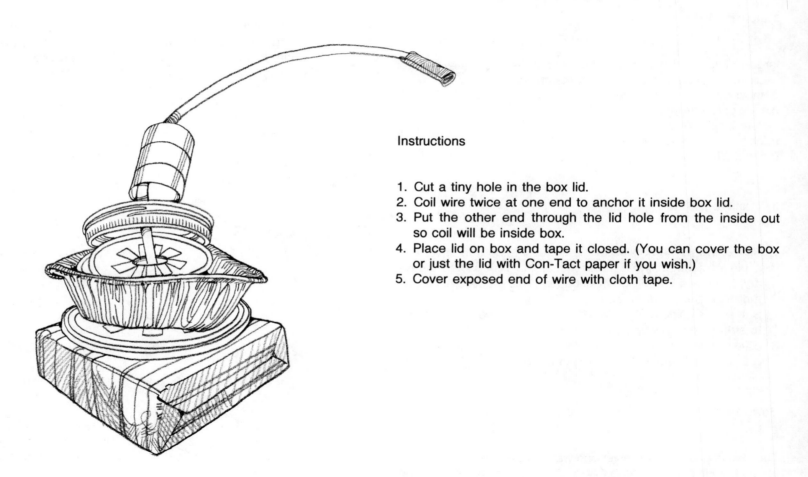

Instructions

1. Cut a tiny hole in the box lid.
2. Coil wire twice at one end to anchor it inside box lid.
3. Put the other end through the lid hole from the inside out so coil will be inside box.
4. Place lid on box and tape it closed. (You can cover the box or just the lid with Con-Tact paper if you wish.)
5. Cover exposed end of wire with cloth tape.

Things to String on Wire

Materials

1 small foil pan, 4″ in diameter
2 to 3 plastic lids
empty toilet-paper roll, cut in half, edges bound with cloth tape
screw-on part of home-canning lid
"donuts" cut out of cardboard
cloth tape

Instructions

1. In the middle of the pan and lids cut a hole about ¾″ in diameter.
2. Line each hole with small pieces of cloth tape slit every ¼″ to cover any sharp edges.

How to Use

Present all objects already on wire. Let your toddler pull them off. Then show her how to poke wire through a hole. The objects with wide holes in the center can be dropped onto the wire. Some objects not centered may teeter at the end of the wire in an amusing way.

Variation

Here's another way to duplicate the pleasure a toddler gets from stringing. If you have an old percolator coffeepot, your toddler will enjoy threading the metal spindle through the hole in the grounds basket.

60. Moon Craters

Reason for Toy

These holes invite poking, an action toddler fingers are accustomed to. Each curious prod is met with a different texture. Just the ticket to sustain interest!

Materials

1 empty egg carton
heavyweight cardboard
bits of foil, smooth fabric, terrycloth, fake fur, or velvet, sandpaper, cotton
brightly colored cloth tape, 1½" wide
Elmer's Glue-All

Instructions

1. On the underside of the carton cut holes in about 5 of the egg compartments.
2. From heavy cardboard cut 5 circles about 1½" in diameter. Glue a bit of cotton on one; a piece of rough sandpaper on another; some crinkled-up foil on the third; smooth fabric on the fourth; and terrycloth, velvet, or fur on the last.
3. Wedge these circles tightly into the indentations for the eggs so that the textures to be felt are positioned about ¼" to ½" below the holes.
4. Take thin strips of cloth tape and tape the circles in place (a).
5. Glue carton closed and wrap cloth tape around the seam. Snip tape to fit contours (b).

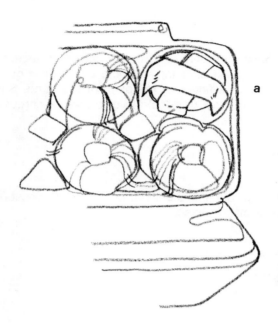

a

How to Use

First give your toddler a chance to play digital games of his own invention with this toy. Later you may describe the textures as he feels them: rough, smooth, soft, furry. Talking about toys builds the vocabulary of words your child understands (and will later say).

b

61. Lazy Susan

Reason for Toy

Toddlers like to spin wheels. The decoration of this tray makes rotating it an exciting visual experience.

Materials

an old lazy Susan or an inexpensive plastic one (from hardware store, sold for inside kitchen cabinets)
1½"-long section of empty paper-towel roll
2 tongue depressors
fabric scraps: a couple of circles and a wedge shape
2 ribbons or 6"-long fabric strips
spray can lid
plastic animals or people (optional)
brightly colored cloth tape, ¾" wide
cloth tape, 1½" wide, or fabric strips
large paper clip
Elmer's Glue-All

Instructions

1. Decorate the paper-towel roll with cloth tape or a strip of fabric glued on. Glue roll near the rim of the lazy Susan.
2. Glue the tongue depressors together, catching 2 ribbons or fabric strips between them at one end. When this construction is dry, glue the tongue depressors, standing up, to the inside of the roll. Use a liberal amount of glue and clamp in place until dry with a large paper clip.
3. Glue fabric scraps to the lazy Susan. Make a couple of V shapes on lazy Susan with the cloth tape.
4. If your lazy Susan is wood, you can also glue a spray can lid and a couple of small toys like animal figures to it. (These will not adhere well, however, to a plastic surface.)

How to Use

Lay lazy Susan on table or floor, not carpet. If necessary, show child how to get it spinning, pushing on the rim or on one of the objects with a finger or the palm of the hand. She can set on miniature animals or people to give them a carousel ride.

Safety Note

Don't use popsicle sticks instead of tongue depressors, as they would break off too easily.

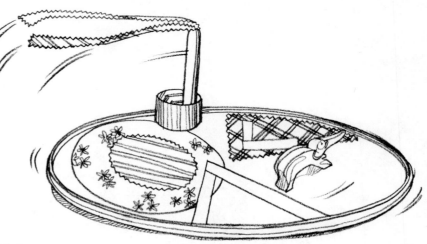

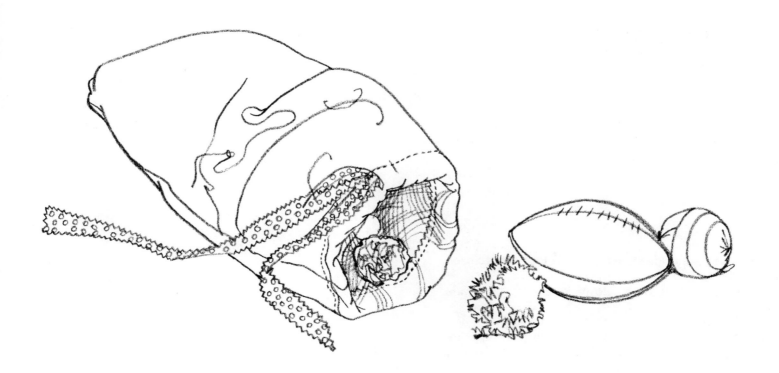

62. Ball Bag

Reason for Toy

Child development researchers have discovered that the ball is the single most popular toy of the 1- to 2-year-old population. These balls vary in appearance and behavior. One wobbles, another rolls far, a third rolls only a short way, still another stops dead when tossed. Plenty of action for toddler observation!

Your sports fan may pile his collection into his lap and throw or roll them to you one at a time. He may click that shiny foil ball and Ping-Pong ball together for a castinet sound. He may enjoy the staccato tapping of the Ping-Pong ball bounced along the kitchen floor.

Bag

Materials

piece of fabric, 9″ × 28″
ribbon, 36″ long
large safety pin
thread

Instructions

1. Fold fabric in half, right sides together, and stitch sides closed. Turn right side out.
2. Turn the fabric inside at the top to make a hem 1½″ wide. Stitch it.
3. On outside front of hem make a ¾″ slit vertically.
4. Attach safety pin to end of ribbon and feed it through the slit around inside of hem and out again to make drawstring. Remove pin.

Balls

Materials

sheet of aluminum foil
lengthy piece of yarn
old argyle sock
filling (cotton balls or polyester pillow stuffing)
string

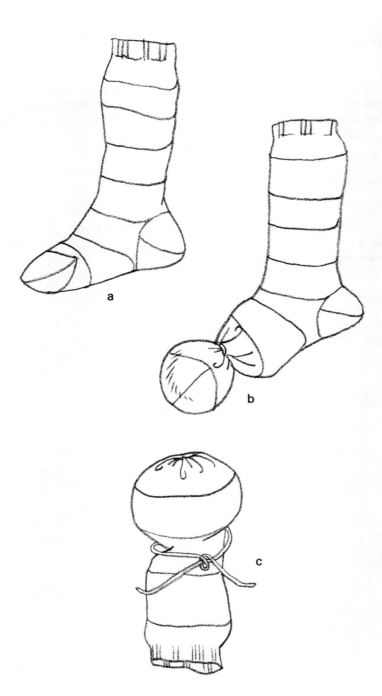

Instructions

Foil Ball:

1. Crumple a good-sized piece of aluminum foil.
2. Wad it together tightly to make a solid shiny ball, 1½″ in diameter or larger.

Puff Ball:

1. Wrap yarn loosely around your palm 100 times.
2. Slip yarn off and tie it tightly around the middle with another piece of yarn.
3. Cut through loops at both ends.
4. Fluff out into a ball shape.

Sock Ball:

1. Stuff toe of sock (a) with filling.
2. Wrap a string around sock foot, gathering material to form ball shape (b). Tie tightly closed.
3. Turn sock inside out and tie closed again on other side of ball (c).
4. Turn right side out over ball and, instead of tying, cut off whatever leg is left and sew opening closed, gathering it.

How to Use

Also add to bag a tennis ball, toy golf ball, Ping-Pong ball, Wiffle ball, small foam football, and soft rubber ball. Vary the contents of the bag, not giving all at once, but adding a new one occasionally as a surprise.

63. Plug the Hole

Reason for Toy

With this stopper, your child can practice her skill at fitting one object into another. For a while the stopper will be left half in and half out of the hole. Wedging it in precisely will later give her a sense of achievement.

Materials

empty 16-ounce white plastic frozen orange juice container
red yarn or string, 15″ long
rubber basin stopper, 1⅜″ to 1½″ in diameter
cloth tape, ¾″ wide
steel wool

Instructions

1. Using steel wool and soapy water, rub writing off container.
2. In the bottom of the container cut a hole 1½″ in diameter and punch a tiny hole next to it with ice pick or knife point (a).
3. Take yarn or string and poke it through the tiny hole with the ice pick or knife point. Draw it through far enough temporarily to make a knot.
4. Tie a large tight knot at the end of the yarn on the inside of the container so it can't pull back through hole.
5. Tie rubber stopper to the other end of the yarn.
6. Cut a strip of cloth tape, slitting it every ¼″ or so and line the edge of the hole with it.

How to Use

Hand this toy to your child with stopper in place. The metal ring handle, which swings back and forth, invites inspection. Examining an object precedes performing a skill with it such as plugging the hole.

Variation

Any container with an opening such as this one can also serve as a depository for a lightweight toy golf ball or a group of Ping-Pong balls. Drop them in, watch them roll out.

64. Mechanism Board

Reason for Toy

If you judged career destinies by the aptitudes and interests of kids from 1 to 2 years old, you'd predict all girls and boys would grow up to be mechanics. Toddlers love to work the moving parts of small gadgets, sliding a bolt, zipping up a zipper, unclasping a hook.

Materials

piece of plywood, 9½″ × 17″ × ½″
piece of balsa wood or corrugated cardboard, 6″ × 2¼″
round wide-angle car mirror, 3″ in diameter, with adhesive back
1 swivel castor
sleigh bell, 1½″ in diameter

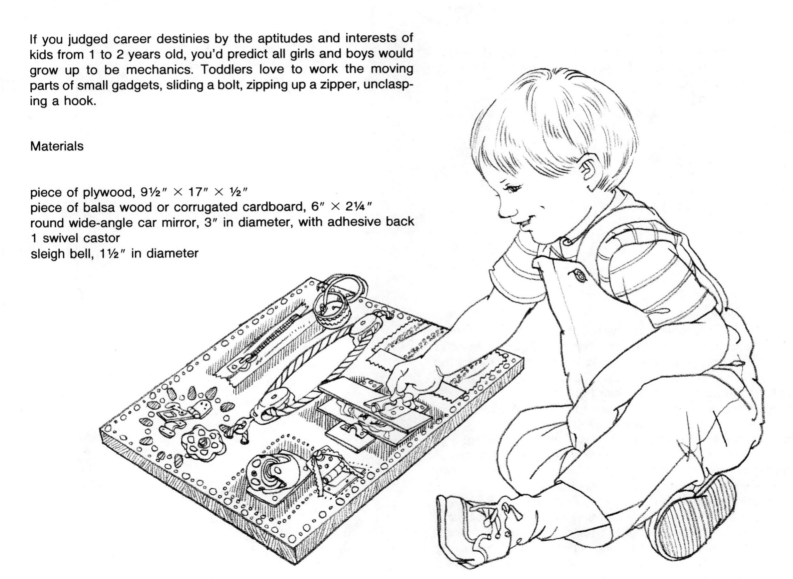

2 swivel eye pulleys
barrel bolt, 2″ long
metal hinge, 1¾″ square
small hasp, with hook latch, plus accompanying nails or screws
outdoor faucet handle
small screw
interestingly shaped hinge
6″ skirt zipper
brightly colored fabric, 4½″ × 5½″ (cut with pinking shears)
cardboard core from a roll of 1½″-wide cloth tape
picture, cut from magazine
mediumweight string
piece of rope or thick twine, 2′ long
narrow ribbon
cloth tape
transparent Con-Tact paper
Elmer's Glue-All
epoxy
acrylic or other nontoxic paints

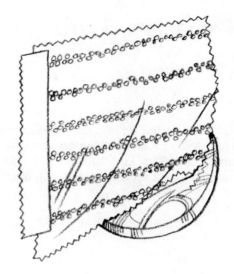

a

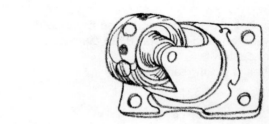

b

Instructions

1. Sand plywood well.
2. Press the mirror onto the board in the lower right corner.
   Cover it with the rectangle of fabric by running a bead of
   glue down one edge of the fabric; glue it to the left of the
   mirror. When glue is dry, add a strip of cloth tape (cut with
   pinking shears) to reinforce joint (a).
3. Epoxy the base of the swivel castor to the board in the lower
   left corner (b). Decorate wheel with dots of paint.
4. With epoxy or glue attach the zipper along upper edge of
   board. (Be careful to put glue only along the very edges of
   the zipper tape.) When you lay it on the board, pinch it slightly
   so the zipper teeth stand up off the board a little.
5. Decorate the cardboard core with some cloth tape cut with
   pinking shears. Epoxy it to the upper right corner of the board.
6. Drill a small hole in upper right corner of the board. Tie sleigh
   bell to the center of a 14″-long string. Thread the string
   through hole and tie it (c). (Bell can hang free or be popped
   into its cardboard core cubbyhole.)

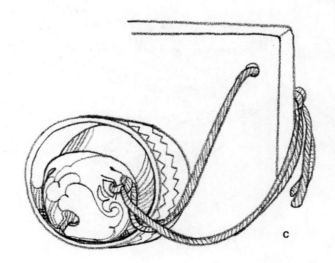

c

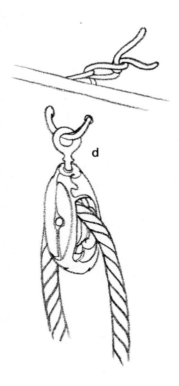

d

7. Drill 2 small holes about ½″ apart at right side of board and 2 more about 10″ toward center of board. With string, tie each pulley to the board, threading string through pulley eye and pair of holes. Feed rope through the pulleys and knot well (d).

8. From the balsa wood or heavy cardboard cut a door, 6″ × 2¼″. Epoxy half the hinge to the inside of the door and the other half to the board. Epoxy the barrel bolt to the door. Glue a small piece of balsa or cardboard to the board right beside the door. It should be the same thickness as the door. To that small piece, epoxy the socket for the bolt to slide into. Place the socket exactly opposite bolt so it slides in easily (e). Behind the door glue a magazine picture. Cover the picture with Con-Tact paper to protect it.

9. Fasten the hasp with hook latch to upper left corner of the board (f). Use the tiny nails and screws that come with the hardware, but make sure they are not so long as to go clear through the plywood board. (If they protrude, use shorter ones.)

10. Below the hasp attach the outdoor faucet handle with a screw to the board. Do not tighten the screw, but leave the head a bit above the board surface so the handle can spin nicely (g).

e

f

11. Between the castor and the door, screw on another hinge with one side loose to flip back and forth. Just for fun you can tie a bow of ribbon on the free side through a screw hole (h).
12. Take acrylic paints and make brightly colored decorative patterns around the devices you've attached to the board.

How to Use

Save this potpourri of gadgetry for a special occasion when other events won't compete for your child's attention. Both Dad and Mom will want to be on hand to watch their toddler discover how to operate each mechanism.

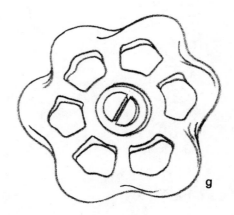

g

Variation

The contrivances displayed on our board are just suggestions. Browse in your hardware or variety stores for other ideas.

Safety Note

Do not mount on board anything with points or sharp edges or small places where little fingers can get pinched. Shun all gadgets, however intriguing, with tiny parts that could break off or be screwed off.

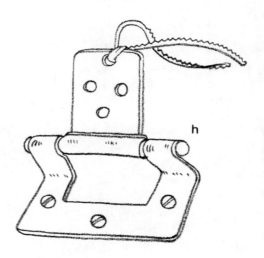

h

65. Covered Wagon

Reason for Toy

Here's a container for treasured objects that is mobile. A doll or a group of favorite things can be taken for a ride. Toddlers enjoy rotating wheels with their fingers, a movement that they can perform when this wagon is upside down.

Materials

shoe box
4 binding head screws and 4 binding posts no more than 1″
   long (½″ if available)
piece of cardboard, heaviest you have
string or ribbon, 40″ long
Con-Tact paper (optional), brightly colored or patterned
cloth tape (optional)
Elmer's Glue-All

Instructions

1. For decorative look, cover shoe box and its lid with Con-Tact paper and tape the edges with cloth tape.
2. On the cardboard, use a glass to draw 8 circles, each 3″ in diameter. Cut them out and spread glue liberally on 4 of them. Glue the other 4 circles to these, making 4 wheels of double-thickness. Let dry.
3. With ice pick or knife point poke 2 holes in one end of the box. Double string and push ends through holes and tie on inside. Tie a slip knot at 6-inch intervals along string handle.
4. Punch a hole in center of each wheel with ice pick or knife point, and in sides of wagon, about 2″ from each end and 3″ to 4″ up from bottom. Enlarge these holes by wiggling pick around, then by inserting tips of scissors and twisting them around in holes.
5. Line up hole of wheel with hole of box. Put binding post through both holes, threading it from outside of wheel to inside of box. Twist the screw into the post, attaching wheel (a). Do this for each wheel. (If posts are too long and wheels too wobbly, add another tiny wheel of cardboard on inside of wagon. Its center hole must line up with holes in box and outside wheel.)

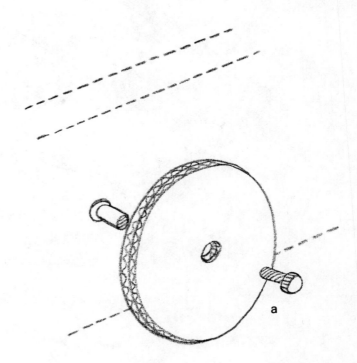

Safety Note

A loop of string is dangerous if a baby can draw it over her head and get it tangled, so be sure to tie knots in this string handle. Bring this toy out when you're playing together.

How to Use

Encourage your daughter to transfer her collection of small objects, or a group of just the similar objects in her collection, from one container (such as the Pail Pal of Chapter Five) to another. In this wagon they can be hidden by the lid or revealed for inspection.

66. White Cat and Friends

Reason for Toy

Hand puppets stimulate language development. A toddler listening to you talk through the puppet will learn new words. A child talking back to his puppet friend will exercise a budding ability to make conversation.

   Hand puppets also stimulate the imagination. Between 1½ and 2 years, toddlers begin to play very simplified make-believe games. You can encourage the ability to pretend when you make the puppet come alive.

Materials

2 pieces of white felt, 8″ × 10″
scraps of felt, in pink, green, and black
Elmer's Glue-All
heavy black thread
a few straight pins

Instructions

1. Cut 2 exactly alike basic puppet shapes out of white felt. Cut 2 white triangle ears. Cut 3 smaller pink triangles for inside of ears.
2. Glue pink triangle on the white ones.
3. Pin the 2 puppet pieces together and pin the ears in place at top edge.
4. Sew puppet on the machine or by hand all around the outside of the cat, catching the ears on the head as you go. Leave bottom open for your hand.
5. Cut out green circles and smaller black ones for eyes, a nose circle of pink felt, and a mouth shape of pink too. (A paper punch makes neat small circles.) Glue these onto face.
6. Whiskers can be made of heavy thread. Sew loops near mouth, then cut with scissors.

How to Use

Put your hand inside the puppet. The index finger goes into head, the thumb into one arm, and the middle finger in the other. As you talk (or purr), you can make the white cat point to things, clap hands, wave bye-bye, shake hands with your baby, or stroke her cheek.

The white cat can ask your toddler to do things, such as point to her whiskers or pet her.

Variations

Many different animal or person characters can be made from this basic puppet design. All you have to do is change the shape and size of the ears, eyes, and mouth, or add hair or a hat. If your child enjoys this cat, make more puppets, copying the sketches.

67. Jack-in-the-Box

Reason for Toy

This toy teaches a baby that someone who disappears can reappear. Such a toy is perhaps reassuring. It imparts the sense of drama and delight anyone experiences when losing a friend and finding him again.

Its featured attraction is the hinged action of the lid, making it a lot easier to open than the commercial jack-in-the-box with a crank handle.

The Box

Materials

strong box, about 6″ × 6″ × 3″, or stiff corrugated cardboard
   from a carton whose sides are at least 12″ × 12″
brightly colored cloth tape

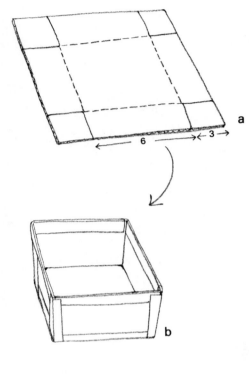

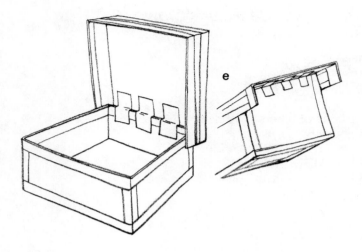

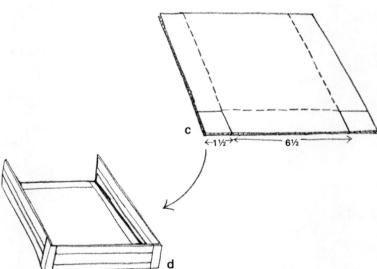

Instructions

If you do not have the right size of box, construct one as follows:
1. Start with a 12"-square piece of cardboard. Cut away all corner pieces 3" × 3". Score along lines forming a 6" square (a). (Score on the side you wish to make the outside of your box.)
2. Bend up the cardboard along the scored lines until the sides meet (b) and tape them together to form a box.
3. Tape all rough edges.
4. You have to make a special lid whether you found a box or made one. Cut a cardboard square 9½" × 9½" and cut away 2 corner pieces 1½" × 1½" (c).
5. Score along lines on 3 sides as shown in figure (c).
6. Bend only the 3 sides and tape together where they meet. Tape rough edges (d).
7. Tape the lid to the box inside and outside (e) so it opens in a hinged fashion. The back of the lid extends past the box. A push on it provides the leverage necessary to open the box.

Jack, the Clown

Materials

1 tennis ball
1 or 2 pieces of different fabrics
3 pipe cleaners
yarn
thread
acrylic or other nontoxic paint
Elmer's Glue-All

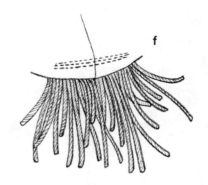

Instructions

1. Cut a tennis ball in half and paint a face on fuzzy side of 1 half with acrylic paint.
2. Cut out 2 small triangles of fabric to make a pointed hat for the face. Sew triangles together, right sides facing, but don't sew bottom edge of hat. Turn right side out.
3. Sew yarn hair to the inside of the hat at both sides (f).
4. Sew a pipe cleaner to inside rim of hat. Bend the pipe cleaner and it will make the hat cock to the side.
5. Glue hat and hair to head.
6. To make a body, cut out matching "body" shapes (g) from the fabric. Sew together (right sides facing) all around except at neck. Turn right-side out.
7. Twist 2 pipe cleaners together and put one inside each arm so you can bend the arms forward (h).
8. Glue the back of the body across shoulders to bottom third of lid (near hinge) so skirt falls into box.
9. With plenty of glue, adhere the head (with hat and hair) to the box lid, covering neck of body.

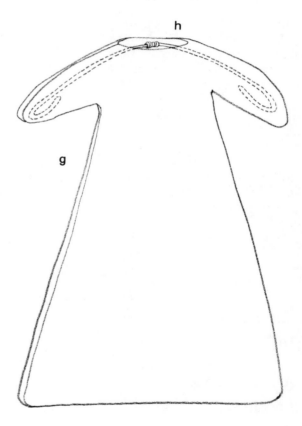

How to Use

Openings and closings can be accompanied by your exclamations of "Hi" and "Goodbye," "Peek-a-boo," or "Where's the clown?" A few little toys can be stored inside on the clown's lap.

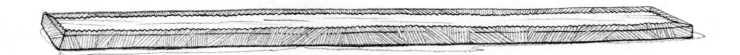

68. Balance Beam

Reason for Toy

Once a toddler is a well-balanced walker, he might enjoy a little challenge to that walking skill. Learning to negotiate this balance beam gives your junior gymnast 1 more accomplishment to crow about. Toddlers thrive on applause or cheers for "work" well done, as you undoubtedly notice.

Materials

1 wooden board, 1″ thick and 4″ wide × 5′ long
2 long strips of fabric, each 2″ × 5′4″ (use fabric scraps cut with pinking shears or fabric tape)
sandpaper
Elmer's Glue-All

Instructions

1. Sand the board so there is no possibility of splinters.
2. Cover edges of board with fabric. Smear a layer of glue along edges and a ½″ stripe of glue on top and bottom near edges. Adhere fabric for decorative border.

How to Use

Lay beam on the floor and let your baby approach it in his own time and way. He may have fun just standing on it at first, and getting on and getting off it. Later you can walk on it to demonstrate. If he wants to walk or side step on it and is quite unsteady, you can walk behind him with your hands under his shoulders.

Variation

When he is very good at maneuvering the beam, raise it 1″ or 2″ by putting a book under each end. The beam also makes a good street for little cars.

69. Jewel Box

Reason for Toy

These tiny bean bags have both visual and tactile appeal. If you use 12 different, brightly colored and tiny-figured fabrics they gleam inside their egg-carton compartment like crown jewels. Some feel squishy, others lumpy and bumpy. The dozen jewels become delightful portable objects to be put in and taken out and fitted into other containers or pockets.

Materials

empty egg carton
12 different fabric scraps (include some shiny, suckable vinyl)
polyester pillow stuffing
dried beans of various sizes and split peas
thread

Instructions

1. Plan about 8 different shapes for your 12 bean bags: square, rectangular, round, heart-shaped, diamond-shaped, oval, triangular, wedge-shaped.
2. Cut out 2 pieces of fabric for each shape. Shapes should be approximately 2½″ to 3½″ in width at widest point.
3. With thin fabrics, put right sides together and stitch almost all the way around circumference ¼″ from edge, leaving an opening of about 1¼″. Turn right-side out. Fill some with polyester, some with split peas, and others with big or little beans. Then stitch opening closed.
4. With stiff fabrics, put wrong sides together. Stitch almost all the way around circumference ¼″ from outside edge, leaving an opening of 1¼″. Stuff some with polyester, others with beans or peas. Stitch opening closed.
5. Egg carton need not be decorated.

How to Use

After your toddler plays several days with this toy as is, give her an ice-cube tray or muffin tin along with the jewel box. Her natural inclination will be to transfer the bean bags from the egg carton to the equally inviting rows of compartments in the tray or tin.

70. Puzzle for Problem-Solvers

Reason for Toy

Your baby is ready to sort shapes. He will like finding the right hole for each shape; he has a built-in tendency to enjoy such problem-solving. However, the shapes and the frame are also pleasing objects just to handle and play with in an unstructured way.

Materials

Use the same materials as listed in the patterns called First Puzzle (Chapter Five) and Second Puzzle (earlier in this chapter).

Instructions

1. Follow the directions for First Puzzle in cutting and laminating cardboard and taping edges, but make 2, 3, or 4 different shapes depending on your baby's ability. Make a sun, tree, and house shapes. (The diameter of the sun should be at least 1½" wide, so there is no danger of swallowing it.)
2. With felt-tip pen draw grass, path, and cloud on frame.
3. When taping around shapes and the insides of holes, use 1"-wide tape and snip it at least every ¼" along both sides. Then you can spread the tabs apart inside curves, overlapping them around front and back sides of puzzle.

How to Use

Schedule one-on-one times almost daily when you can be alone with your baby, especially if there are other children in the house. Puzzles, matching games like Lotto, and shape- and size-sorting activities provide magical moments when you can have the joy of watching your baby learn to think.

Variation

To create another puzzle, use your plastic cookie cutters—star, heart, gingerbread man. In laminated cardboard frame, cut holes which correspond to their shapes.

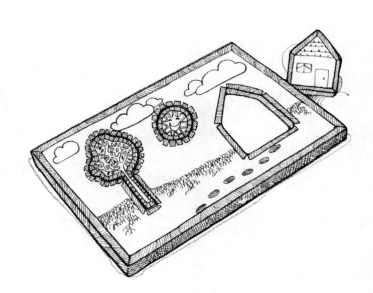

71. Sound Experiment

Reason for Toy

The variety of sounds produced when your child shakes these canisters gives her the incentive to listen closely. Gradually she'll get interested in comparing the different rattles. She may become aware of different weights too. She'll be exercising her capacity to notice similarities and differences.

Your child can practice mastery skills with these, setting them up in a row, knocking them over and rolling them.

Materials

6 empty film canisters, metal or plastic (1 transparent if possible)
1 tablespoon of unpopped popcorn
1 penny
a button
a few metal clothing snaps
silver cake-decorating candies
safety pins
1 barette
1 bolt
epoxy

Instructions

1. Fill each canister with a different item or group of items. You could put a penny in the first canister; a button and a few snaps in the second; unpopped popcorn in the third; safety pins in the fourth; a bolt, barette, and safety pin all in the sixth. If you have just 1 see-through canister, put the shiny silver candies in there.
2. Spread epoxy on threads where lids screw or snap on. Attach lids as tightly as possible and wipe away excess epoxy. Let dry overnight.

How to Use

To help your toddler become aware of her valuable sense of hearing, talk about listening to the sounds these rattlers make, as well as to other sounds around the house. *Loud* and *soft*, or *noisy* and *quiet* are words you can use often to teach the concepts they describe.

Safety Note

Keep checking that glue on lids is holding.

72. Periscopes

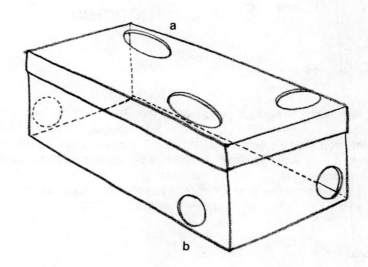

Reason for Toy

Tots like to fit one thing into another; here the bell fits into the mouth of the tube. Tots like to follow the paths of moving objects; the bell rolls out of a tube and along the floor. They like variety; each tube shoots out the bell in a different direction. Finally, they like disappearance and reappearance (as in that old standby peek-a-boo); with this toy, the bell disappears down the tube and emerges on the other side of the box.

Materials

shoe box, 5½″ × 9½″
3 empty paper-towel rolls, or similar cardboard tubes
large sleigh bell, 1½″ in diameter, or small ball
Con-Tact paper, brightly colored or patterned
colored cloth tape or masking tape

Instructions

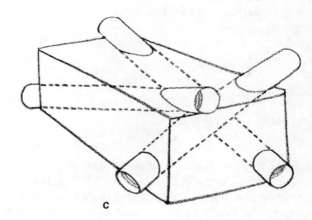

1. With a sharp mat knife or scissors, cut 3 oval holes (a) in the shoe box lid. These should be about 3″ long and 1½″ wide. Each tube will be slotted through the box on a diagonal so bell or ball will roll down and out.
2. Cut 3 round holes (b) in side of box, each one opposite one of the ovals. These should be 1½″ in diameter.
3. Cover box with Con-Tact paper, cutting holes in paper where there are holes in box.
4. Poke tubes through holes, trimming lengths of tubes if necessary to make box lie flat (c).
5. Working with short strips of tape about 3½″ long, slit strips every half inch. Tape each tube to box where it emerges from hole (d).

6. Cut off an end of one roll, so you have a ring 1″ wide. Slit at intervals a piece of cloth tape and fasten the ring to the top of the box as a holder for the bell.

How to Use

After your child has played with this on the floor, place the box near the edge of a coffee table. Now when the ball comes out the tube, it will plummet through the air before rolling across the floor. Expect such demonstrations of the principle of gravity to provoke shrieks of delight.

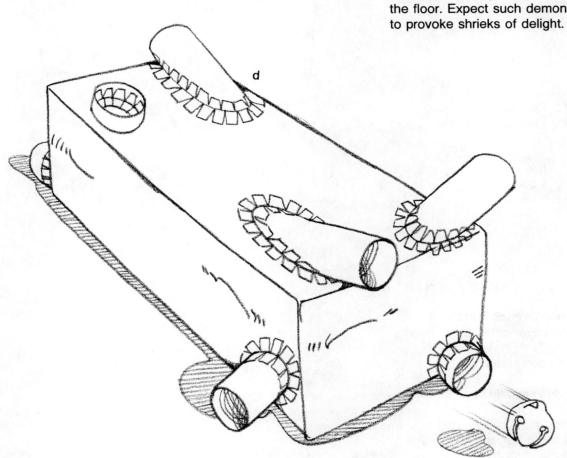

73. Light-Up Cylinders

Reason for Toy

Easy-to-work simple mechanisms give toddlers a thrill. The ability to turn darkness into light is heady stuff! If you shop around, you can find a flashlight with a switch that moves from the "off" to "on" position with a gentle push.

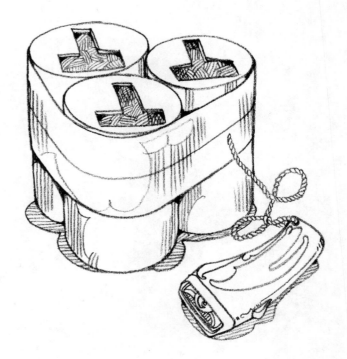

Materials

3 empty cylindrical salt cartons
Con-Tact paper, brightly colored or patterned
3 pictures cut from magazine or cereal box advertisement
small, easy-to-switch-on flashlight
cloth tape, 1½" wide
heavyweight string or yarn
acrylic or other nontoxic paint, in bright color

Instructions

1. Cut off the bottom of each salt carton, slicing it about 1" from the end.
2. Glue a picture inside the cut-off end of each carton (a).
3. Tape the end back on again and cover sides and bottoms of cartons with Con-Tact paper.
4. Cut a T-shaped hole in the top of each carton.
5. Paint the tops.
6. Run a strip of tape 23" long around the middle of all 3 cartons, binding them together.
7. If possible, tie string onto the flashlight. (Our light had a hole to thread the string through.) Tie the other end of the string around one of the cartons above the cloth tape.
8. Now run another length of cloth tape around all 3 cartons above where you tied on the flashlight.

How to Use

Present this toy toward evening in a dimly lit room. Flash the light into the keyhole openings and invite your toddler to peek at the pictures. Play together with this toy until your child can work the flashlight himself. Otherwise, the fun could be spoiled by the frustration of not being able to push the switch.

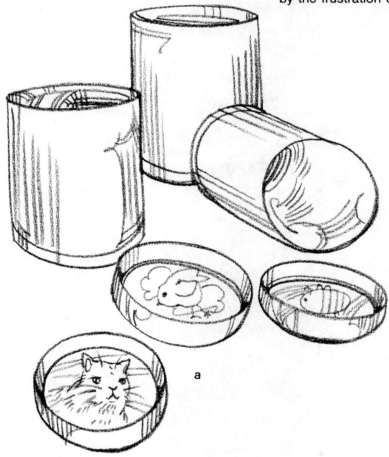

a

74. Matching Pictures and Objects

Reason for Toy

Your home is a think tank in which to play problem-solving games. This exercise in matching entails scanning the objects and the pictures and sorting out those that go together.

Materials

7 plastic tumblers or margarine tubs
7 small magazine pictures or illustrations from the sides of food packages
7 corresponding concrete objects, such as an orange, apple, keys, ball, cork, ribbon tied in a bow, spool of thread, toothbrush, teabag

Instructions

Paste the picture of each object in the bottom of a tumbler or tub.

How to Use

Present your child with a few tumblers and the corresponding objects. At first, don't require him to match them. Dropping in the objects randomly and then taking them out will be fun; gradually your child may notice the correlation. Or you may show him how to play the game in a low-key way. "Which cup do the keys go in? That's right, with the picture of the keys."

A near 2-year-old can begin with 3 or 4 tumblers and go on quickly to 7 or 8 choices. A younger baby could start with 2 cups and 2 objects and incorporate more into his game very gradually. Feel free to hint whenever help would be welcome. Labeling verbally the objects and pictures will build vocabulary and aid in completing the task.

75. Size Trials

Reason for Toy

When your child nears 2 years of age, she is becoming more and more of a thinker. She can be aware of various options and choose one without necessarily having to try them out manually before making the correct choice. You may notice that at some point your child can judge size mentally without going through a trial fitting operation.

Materials

2 or 3 sturdy containers with tops that are easy to press on and pull off (try for different sizes of the same style of container—perhaps a gallon, quart, and pint from an ice cream shop)
printed fabric or patterned Con-Tact paper
Elmer's Glue-All

Instructions

1. Cover sides of containers by gluing a length of fabric or adhering Con-Tact paper.
2. Cut a circle of fabric or Con-Tact and adhere it to top of lid.

How to Use

Let your child practice fitting just the large lid to the large container. Then introduce another lid and have her choose which of the 2 lids fits that container. Perhaps place a toy car or animal inside and say, "Cover up the car." Bring out the second container now. When she can discriminate between the 2 containers and 2 lids, complicate the task with a third container and lid. Help her to learn the concepts of "big" and "small" by using these words often.

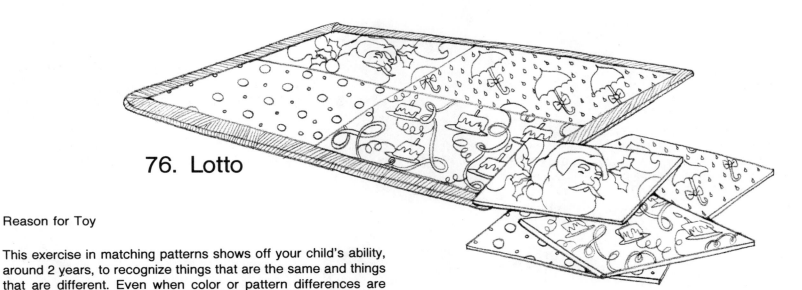

76. Lotto

Reason for Toy

This exercise in matching patterns shows off your child's ability, around 2 years, to recognize things that are the same and things that are different. Even when color or pattern differences are subtle, a child who accumulates experience playing matching games can notice the discrepancies.

Materials

2 shirt cardboards
4 different gift-wrap papers (1 plain, 3 with easy-to-distinguish figures such as Santas, babies, Donald Ducks)
transparent Con-Tact paper
cloth tape (optional)
pencil
black felt-tip pen
Elmer's Glue-All

Instructions

1. With pencil and ruler divide 1 cardboard into 4 parts.
2. On each part glue a different piece of paper cut to fit square. Outline between the squares with felt-tip pen. This makes your Lotto board.
3. Cut the second piece of cardboard into 4 individual squares the size of those on your Lotto board.
4. Cover each small square with a piece of paper that matches one of the squares on your board.
5. Cover board and 4 squares with Con-Tact paper for added durability and good looks. The board can also be bound with cloth tape.

How to Use

The point of a Lotto game is to lay the individual cards onto the board squares which they match. Don't present all the little cards at once. They can be confusing. Keep 2 out of sight, and lay 2 near the Lotto board. "Where do the babies go?" you can ask. Or, "Put the Santa faces together." If he puts a card on a wrong square, just say "No" and shake your head till he makes the match. He'll soon catch on.

Variation

Glue on other gift-wrap papers with differences in design that are more subtle. Make another board with 6 or 8 squares. A sophisticated board could be made with sheets of construction paper that vary only slightly in color.

77. Smell Test

Reason for Toy

This game exercises 1 of the 5 senses not often used in play. A near 2-year-old will enjoy the act of sniffing whether she tries to match the smells or not. Comparing whiffs helps her become aware of similarities and differences. She will want to share the fun with Mom, Dad, or even pet!

Materials

3 pairs of salt and pepper shakers with good-sized holes
6 balls of cotton
some sweet and savory substances, such as perfume; after-shave lotion; mouthwash; vanilla, almond, lemon, or mint extract; vinegar; garlic or onion juice

Instructions

1. Saturate each cotton ball with a few drops of one of the substances and put it inside a shaker.
2. Fill each shaker differently or, for a matching game, fill each pair with the same smell.

How to Use

Sniff one shaker, hand it to toddler, and say, "Smell it. It's sweet." Then sniff another shaker and perhaps say, "Ooh! Smell this. It's sour." Your child may not be able to match smells until after 2 years of age, but she will notice contrasting odors.

Serendipity List

According to Webster's dictionary, *serendipity* means "the gift of finding valuable or agreeable things not sought for." Your baby possesses this gift. As she explores her home she will find many valuable or agreeable objects not intended to be toys. However, to her they may have great intrinsic play value. As long as household gadgets and objects are safe and durable, they are certainly as acceptable as commercial or homemade toys.

You can enrich your child's playtimes by becoming aware of things in your home which are appropriate for these early stages of development. Then your baby will not have to rely on an infrequent chance discovery of some commonplace utensil that could be such fun for her to examine.

The following lists give you suggestions of possible items you may have in stock. If you have a new home sparsely supplied with odds and ends, perhaps there's a grandmother's house you could raid. If you have a toy budget, you may rather spend it at places that aren't toy stores. Other possibilities are factory outlets, plumbing or electrical supply stores, appliance repair stores which have molded plastic spare parts, and hardware departments of discount stores.

Kitchen gadgets

plastic cookie cutter
popsicle mold
egg separator
slotted spoon
wooden or plastic mixing spoon
meat baster
funnels (2 sizes for nesting)
strainers (2 sizes for nesting)
eggbeater for frothing soapsuds in bathtub (with parent supervising)
rubber spatula
wooden mallet head (for tenderizing
   meat)
tea infuser
flexible rubber disk (for twisting lids open)

melon baller
bottle stopper
plastic juice squeezer
flour, sugar, tea canisters with easy-to-put-in-place lids
bendable straw
colander
measuring spoons
measuring cups
hinged metal implement (for twisting lids open)
pastry brush
very large cake-decorating nozzle and pastry bag
individual plastic ice-cube mold

Household objets d'art

padlock
latch on briefcase
latch on trunk
door bolt or latch
plastic tubing
empty plastic squeeze bottles
3"-long aluminum bolt
toilet-paper holder with spring center core (not the kind with a metal spring that could come out)
ottoman or low stool
bolster, cushion, pillow
unbreakable mirror (camping equipment, auto)
plastic lazy Susan (for kitchen cabinet)
short telephone wire, unplugged and coiled
rubber disk for stopping tub drain
electric curlers detached from appliance
clothespin
screwdriver handle (without interchangeable parts)
pleated hand fan

pots, pans, and lids (especially with shiny copper bottoms)
flashlight
blinking Christmas-tree lights any time of year (with parental supervision)
napkin ring
sturdy plastic bracelet
large S hook
small C clamp
vacuum cleaner attachment (for cleaning crevices)
small brush (for cleaning fingernails)
shoehorn
bird-call whistle
dinner bell
roll handle (for carrying packages)
rolls of masking tape, different sizes
rolls of cloth tape, different colors
bathroom plastic drinking cup
toothbrush
empty plastic cosmetic jars and bottles for traveling
telephone cradling device, with nuts and bolts removed
dispenser for roll of stamps (from Post Office)
soap dish
cassette tape box
giant plastic paper clip
key ring
Band-Aid can with flip-top lid
dispenser for Towelettes (screw-on lid has snap-on top in center)
rainy-day plastic front hall runner (for baby to crawl on)
desk organizer (small plastic box with sliding drawers)
desk accessories
plastic or leather luggage tag
metronome (attach yarn fluff ball or bow to end of stick; parent must supervise)
tape recorder (with supervision)
record player (with supervision)

Wastebasket finds

typewriter reels
film cans
cardboard cores from tape rolls
milk cartons of various sizes
plastic lids from spray cans
mailing tubes
crates or cartons that home appliances
   are delivered in
old rubber windshield wiper blades
   (springy)
small cardboard boxes
tissue boxes
rubber gloves, cleansed of any detergent
shirt cardboards
cardboard collar stiffeners
cardboard juice cans with snap-on lids
old deck of cards
plastic baby food jars

Left to right: Karen Kalkstein, Kent Garland Burtt, Eulala Conner

About the Authors

Kent Garland Burtt

Kent Garland Burtt, a freelance writer, has written many articles on early childhood education, family life, and parenting for *The Christian Science Monitor.* She has also contributed to *The New York Times,* edited teacher-training materials, and collaborated on a book titled *Save the Children.* After studying with Burton L. White at Harvard's Institute on Educating the Infant and Toddler, Ms. Burtt developed and taught a course for parents in practical ways to stimulate the development of their child's intelligence. She lives in New York City with the youngest of her four children and spends weekends in Connecticut.

Karen Kalkstein

Karen Kalkstein is an art teacher, a potter, and the owner of a batik T-shirt business. She teaches after-school art classes privately and at The Mead School in Greenwich, Connecticut. She comes from California and now lives in Stamford, Connecticut, with her husband, son, and daughter.

Eulala Conner

Eulala Conner illustrates children's books and educational materials. She grew up in Florida, worked in Los Angeles, and now lives with her husband in Westport, Connecticut. She has a daughter and a son.